WITHDRAWN
HARVARD LIBRARY
WITHDRAWN

THE METAPHYSICS OF COOPERATION

A Study of F.D. Maurice

VIBS

Volume 84

Robert Ginsberg
Executive Editor

Associate Editors

G. John M. Abbarno
Mary-Rose Barral
H. G. Callaway
Rem B. Edwards
Rob Fisher
Dane R. Gordon
J. Everet Green
Heta Häyry
Matti Häyry
Richard T. Hull

Joseph C. Kunkel
Vincent L. Luizzi
Alan Milchman
George David Miller
Michael H. Mitias
Peter A. Redpath
Alan Rosenberg
Arleen Sailes
John R. Shook
Alan Soble

John R. Welch

THE METAPHYSICS OF COOPERATION

A Study of F.D. Maurice

Steven Schroeder

Amsterdam - Atlanta, GA 1999

BX
5199
.M3
S37
1999

∞ The paper on which this book is printed meets the requirements of "ISO 9706:1994, Information and documentation - Paper for documents - Requirements for permanence".

ISBN: 90-420-0776-1
©Editions Rodopi B.V., Amsterdam - Atlanta, GA 1999
Printed in The Netherlands

This book is dedicated to my father, Herbert Schroeder, in gratitude for the inspiration of his quiet courage.

CONTENTS

FOREWORD by Gary Dorrien		ix
PREFACE		xiii
ACKNOWLEDGMENTS		xv
ONE	Puzzled Into Silence	1
	1. A Victorian Life	1
	2. A Little English Church History	2
	3. Lines of Dissent	7
	4. Holy Water for Bourgeois Consciences	11
	5. Intersecting Genealogies	14
	6. Historical Boundaries, Historical Fictions	16
	7. Three Revolutions	22
	8. Diggers	26
TWO	A Circle of Friends	29
	1. A Literary Life	29
	2. Common Ground	31
	3. A System of Philosophy	36
	4. Essential Poetry	40
	5. A Contribution to the Formation of an Age	42
THREE	A System That Is All Door	49
	1. A Universal Church	49
	2. The Spirit, the Body, the Communion of Saints	58
	3. Depth Theology	61
	4. The Union of Godhead with Human Flesh	69
FOUR	The Fever of the Miscellaneous Man	73
	1. The Shape of the City Itself	73
	2. Learning and Working	76
	3. A Practice of Freedom	78
	4. Time, Social Theory, and Educational Practice	80

FIVE	Conclusion	85
NOTES		87
BIBLIOGRAPHY		93
ABOUT THE AUTHOR		99
INDEX		101

FOREWORD

His Anglican admirers aside, Frederick Denison Maurice (1805-1872) is often remembered as a prototype of Karl Marx's image of the Christian Socialist as a sprinkler of holy water on bourgeois heartburn. As an influence on modern theology, Samuel Taylor Coleridge is often remembered for his inspiring impact on a host of American transcendentalists and liberals in the 1830s and 1840s, especially Ralph Waldo Emerson and Horace Bushnell. Steven Schroeder offers a richer picture of Maurice in the present work, casting his thought as a still-instructive blend of liberal-leaning incarnational theology and cooperativist social theory. Along the way, he also makes a compelling case for reading Coleridge's *Aids to Reflection* as a rationale for an experientialist form of Anglican orthodoxy.

The links between these seminal thinkers were biographical and theological, as Schroeder shows. Coleridge was a liberal Unitarian in his early career, but in later life he sought to provide a new philosophical basis for what became the "Broad Church Movement" in English Anglicanism. Appropriating the Kantian distinction between pure and practical reason, as well as Kant's moral intuitionism, his aphoristic *Aids to Reflection* made a case for the moral and experiential nature of Christian truth that inspired a host of American Emersonians, English and American Unitarians and liberals, and young F.D. Maurice. Son of a Unitarian minister, Maurice was a student at Trinity College, Cambridge, in 1825 when *Aids to Reflection* was published. His refusal to subscribe to the Anglican Thirty-Nine Articles cost him his Trinity degree and fellowship, but in the years that followed, increasingly influenced by Coleridge's religious philosophy, Maurice found his way to mainstream Anglicanism. Like his intellectual hero, his religious thinking was creative, multistranded, liberal-leaning, and provocative; as Schroeder shows, he spent much of his career defending himself from accusations of heresy. Though many others claimed this mantle in mid-nineteenth century England and the United States, the present work contains ample evidence for the judgment that Coleridge's hope for a "true to life" account of Christian truth was distinctively fulfilled in the religious thought of Maurice.

Maurice's theology was a novel blend of classical and modern motifs; at its best, modern Anglicanism has been known for qualities that he embodied and advocated. These include his resistance to dogmatism, his pluralistic, inclusive spirit; his theological emphasis on incarnation; his affirmation of reason; and his insistence that true, spiritually-refined worship is the heart of Christian life and thinking. Other aspects of Maurice's theology that hold significant interest today include his patripassionism, his relational conception of divine reality, and his insistence that Christ's atoning work destroyed not merely the penalty for sin, but the state of estrangement itself between God and humankind. In the generation after his death, Maurice became an icon of Broad Church Anglican orthodoxy on the strength of these themes and his exemplary witness. For most of his career, however, his right to the Christian name was bitterly disputed. Schroeder emphasizes that in 1853 Maurice was dismissed from his position as Professor of English Literature and History at King's College; the main point of contention was his claim that the New Testament concept of "eternity" has nothing to do with time. Maurice's Socialism heightened his vulnerability to religious attack during this critical period, a fact that Schroeder notes in objection to Marx's "holy water" sneer.

The authority given the latter pronouncement by countless historians and other observers is curious. Marx heaped violent invective on nearly everyone who disagreed with him, including hapless followers who failed to keep up with his changes of opinion. He smeared Bakuninian anarchists, Lassallean democratic socialists, and all manner of independent radicals as "castrating reformers," "toads," "vermin," "the emigrant scum," and the like. Though his anarcho-syndicalist conception of socialism had little kinship with the single-party dictatorships later erected in his name, Marx's utopianism about the socialist revolutionary ideal made it possible for several generations of communist thugs to call themselves Marxists. His absurd belief in the "withering away of the state" under socialism was partly responsible for the repugnant connotations that "socialism" acquired in the twentieth century. In the nineteenth century, armed with the assurance of possessing a world-conquering ideology—though he didn't call it that—Marx ridiculed the various reformers, Christian Socialists, and Social Democrats of his time for their moralism and lack of revolutionary militancy. Today it is their successors who sustain whatever remains of the egalitarian hope of democratic socialism.

Socialism is no longer innocent in any form. Most of its dominant images are repulsive. Tens of millions have perished in Communist gulags in the name of building socialism; hundreds of millions have been subjected to brutal poverty and state repression in its name; even in its democratic forms, modern socialism has produced bloated welfare states and dispirited political regimes throughout Western Europe. First appearances aside, all of this is pertinent to the present work. Steven Schroeder implicitly reminds us that there was a cooperativist tradition of Christian Socialism before Socialism became an ideology of economic nationalization and centralized state control, with or without democracy. The Christian Socialist tradition pioneered by Maurice, John Ludlow, and Charles Kingsley was community-based, fellowship-oriented, committed to worker education, and strategically social rather than narrowly political. It was explicitly reformist and grounded in moral principle, as Marx charged. It advocated cooperatives and mixed forms of worker and community ownership in the name of raising the condition of a disenfranchised majority.

With all its limitations, the kind of social Christianity pioneered by Maurice thus prefigured what remains of the democratic socialist vision today, which is the practice of community-building, decentralized economic democracy. One does not read Maurice for guidance on the economics of worker ownership or the merits of public bank strategies, but he remains a valuable witness to the original and enduring meaning of Christian Socialism. "Hence this unfashionable book."

Gary Dorrien
Kalamazoo College

PREFACE

Apologists for Capitalism have enjoyed remarkable success in depicting the Cold War as an apocalyptic struggle between radically divergent economic systems. At the end of the Cold War, they have unilaterally declared Capitalism's victory, aided and abetted by a worldwide embrace of the Market that spans the political spectrum. Where the Market goes without saying, discussion of socialism is largely confined to strategies of containment. The mark of relevant discussion is attention to productivity, efficiency, and Market mechanisms. Economics is a descriptive science, and "value" is a necessary outcome of natural processes. As a result, ethics is a branch of decision-theory that orders given outcomes as best it can and cleans up where natural processes and human weaknesses collide in unfortunate disasters.

In such an atmosphere, description is all, and normative investigation appears vaguely anachronistic. If the Market goes without saying, then railing against it is akin to being a conscientious objector to the law of gravity.

Hence this unfashionable book.

If the Market goes without saying, it is because an important philosophical and theological discussion was sidetracked (not silenced, but marginalized) by the rise of descriptive economics between the middle of the nineteenth century and the middle of the twentieth. This book is a modest contribution to getting back on track by digging, as F.D. Maurice would say, toward the common humanity that is the ground of value.

Digging is a philosophical and theological task which calls, not for another descriptive treatise in economics, but for an essay in philosophy.

An essay, by definition, is an exploration of territory. This one is partly defined by time (its focal point is the nineteenth century), partly by space (its focal point is Britain), and partly by persons (it is concerned especially with F.D. Maurice's contribution to social theory). The first chapter explores the Victorian Age as historical context and background for Maurice's work. The second explores Samuel Taylor Coleridge's thought as philosophical context and background. The third explores a range of Maurice's theological works that spans his entire career. The fourth turns, finally, as Maurice did, to the practice of adult education as the place of social transformation and, more particularly, the contested terrain where "human nature" and human souls are turned to work in the world as persons, not hands.

ACKNOWLEDGMENTS

Thanks to colleagues and students at Capital University's Dayton Center for providing a scholarly community in which research and writing are valued as essential to teaching. Dean Gary Smith provided generous support in the form of a reduced load during the Winter term of 1998. Andy Carlson, Fetneh Ghavami, Mike Hoy, Robin Johnson, and Vic Olsen read and/or listened to bits and pieces of the manuscript over the past two years, as did a number of colleagues from Capital and elsewhere at a meeting of the Ohio Academy of Religion in Columbus in March 1998. Ken Rice read the entire manuscript as it came off the printer and provided perceptive comments and stimulating discussion in our study of the history of British socialism during the Winter 1998 term.

When I arrived at the University of Chicago in the mid-1970s, a refugee of sorts from doctrinal wars in the Lutheran Church-Missouri Synod, Bernie Brown introduced me to a world of Anglican social thought that added a new dimension to my Lutheran reading of Marx. When I returned to Chicago after a brief sojourn at the Episcopal Theological Seminary of the Southwest, he and Robin Lovin guided the study of F.D. Maurice that was the starting point for this book. Darrel Gilbertson enriched my reading further during several intense years of peace education in Amarillo. He read an early draft of the book and offered encouragement, as he so often has in the years that I've known him. Members of Epiphany Lutheran Church in Dayton responded thoughtfully to a presentation of the project and convinced me that the book has an audience beyond the academy.

I'm grateful to my family for unwavering support even when my passion for this work has bordered on obsession. Peggy and Regina, as always, are my best critics. My father, Herbert Schroeder (who is neither a socialist nor an Anglican), after sitting at the kitchen counter into the early hours of a January morning listening to my raving about an obscure Anglican theologian and his contribution to the history of socialism said, "That sounds like a book *I'd* like to read." This, as much as anything else, inspired me to get it done.

One
PUZZLED INTO SILENCE

A small boy puzzled into silence by competing forces in the world around him is a poster child for England's Victorian Age. To enhance the image, transform puzzlement into "proper" adult reserve spread over a literary career composed of fiction and journalism as well as theological treatises, philosophical essays, and sermons. Add a stretch of dissent and an impeccably Radical pedigree; a double dose of Oxbridge followed by ordination in the Church of England; teaching positions at Cambridge and the University of London; and a measure of educational, political, and theological controversy that includes dismissal from an academic post and the founding of new colleges in London for women and working men. Readers primed by popular versions of Freud's late Victorian speculations to expect something scandalous when the cover is turned down will be surprised to find nothing but an extraordinary layering of ordinary things poised between the twentieth century and the Revolution in France. The Age has not lost its power to evoke puzzlement and writing, if not silence: the talking cure put an end to that. But the puzzled silence of our poster child is more properly an extended pause between words carefully considered; the cure and the century it has marked are as eminently Victorian as the genius who concocted it.

1. A Victorian Life

The image of F.D. Maurice as a small boy puzzled into silence belongs to his oldest son and first biographer, Frederick. Frederick Maurice's *Life* of his father is a two-volume work composed in properly Victorian fashion almost entirely of correspondence, a life in letters. Two things, at least, the twentieth century has taught us: we cannot understand language without attending to the silences between words, and letters are among the best places to practice reading between the lines.

Maurice's *Life* begins with a concise history of the English Church. Frederick draws the lines of that history together in his grandfather, Michael Maurice, who was a Unitarian minister. The main lines are drawn in a dispute over church polity: one line is Episcopalian, the other Presbyterian. One line has bishops, the other doesn't. Since the line with bishops is the "established" Church of England, "Presbyterian" becomes equivalent to "other" or "dissenter."

But, particularly in Scotland, this issue was not just a matter of polity. A distinctly Calvinist creed (codified in the Westminster Confession) defined membership in the Scottish Presbyterian church, and identification with that creed became an essential attribute of the name "Presbyterian." Because repudiation of creed had been a mark of dissent since the sixteenth century, this identification became problematic, particularly for Baptists and Unitarians.

In Frederick Maurice's account, the announcement by a "regular" Presbyterian minister that he was a "Socinian," that is, a Unitarian, precipitated a gathering in 1719 of dissenters, including Baptists, Independents, and Presbyterians, the purpose of which was "to advise the congregation of the offending member how to act." By a vote of fifty-seven to fifty-three, the gathering decided not to bind its members by any form of creed, "not even by one simply expressive of a worship of the Trinity."[1] The decision not to bind members by a creed made English Presbyterianism a safe haven for the growing body of Unitarians in the English Church, and, along with the Calvinist emphasis on the sovereignty of God, it created a strong emphasis on God's unity within the English Presbyterian tradition.

According to Frederick's account, toward the end of the eighteenth century, English Presbyterians under the leadership of Joseph Priestley began to formulate a strictly Unitarian creed. The result was that

> a man whose opinions were in all main points orthodox might in the same chapel succeed, or be succeeded by, one under the direct influence of dogmatic Unitarianism; and between these extremes there was a considerable number who, whatever their individual opinions might be on one side or the other, yet adhered to the old Presbyterian tradition, and therefore abstained in the pulpit at least from all doctrinal discussion.[2]

Michael Maurice, at twenty-six, was elected over one of the leaders of the "dogmatic Unitarians" as afternoon preacher in the same chapel where Priestley was already morning preacher. This brought him together with Priestley, but it did not alter his "tone of mind," which was that of the 1719 Presbyterian assembly.

2. A Little English Church History

This laudably concise account is likely to leave readers who have not been initiated into the subtleties of British ecclesiastical history thoroughly disoriented. Though the beginning of the Protestant Reformation is still sometimes pictured as a sudden event spatially and temporally localized in sixteenth-century Germany, it was a spread-out affair with roots in several parts of Europe, including England and Scotland, and in several centuries prior and subsequent to the sixteenth.

Because the English Church was less certain of its "Protestant" than of its English identity, its relationship to Continental theological sources was a matter of dispute. In the sixteenth century, it was a national church with episcopal polity and an already extensive history of controversy regarding the proper relationship between bishops and sovereigns; but the English Church was theologically Catholic, not Lutheran or Calvinist.

Because the English Reformation (even more than other segments of the Protestant Reformation) thoroughly entangled theological developments with the formation of national identities, questions of church polity are of more than passing significance. When the English Church initially separated from Rome under Henry VIII, it retained Roman theology. This separation is generally acknowledged to have had more to do with Henry's marital (and extra-marital) affairs than with any deeply theological differences with Rome. The English Church of the sixteenth century was national, not Protestant, but the separation created a space for development of an English Protestant party. Not surprisingly, that development, too, was along national lines, reaching back first to the pre-Reformation English reformer John Wycliffe (c.1328-1384), a master of Balliol College, Oxford, who translated the New Testament into English, looked to Scripture as the only standard by which to judge doctrine and ceremony, and looked to the State for aid in reforming the Church. All three emphases, English language, Scripture, and the State, were taken up by the English Church in the sixteenth century.

The 1534 Supremacy Act made the English sovereign (Henry VIII at the time) head of the Church, but it did not change the Church's theology. This left an opening in England for the dispute between Catholic and Protestant theologies that was then raging on the Continent. It also paved the way for three parties divided along political and theological lines at the time of Henry's death. One favored no change, an English Church with Roman theology that was effectively a formal recognition of a long history of strong monarchs exercising control over territorial churches through bishops more loyal to the crown than to the papacy. A second favored reinstitution of Papal authority, an English Church with Roman theology and Roman government. A third was distinctly Protestant and favored a church along the Lutheran, Calvinist, or Zwinglian lines then developing on the Continent. The often contentious diversity of that third party combined with the threat to sovereignty posed by the second pushed the first toward a concern with order and uniformity that would have considerable impact on English history.

Bear in mind that English tradition included several notable examples of Church and State balancing one another's power, the martyrdom of Thomas à Becket being perhaps the most famous, and that translation of Scripture had been so controversial in the fourteenth and fifteenth centuries partly because it had the potential to effect a transfer of power from both Church and sovereign to people. A 1549 Act of Uniformity required use of the *Book of Common Prayer* in English for worship. This sharpened the division from Rome but also led to considerable dissatisfaction among the Calvinist and Zwinglian Protestants. To Calvinists and Zwinglians, Archbishop Cranmer's prayer book looked distinctly Roman. To Catholics, it looked distinctly Protestant. Uniformity was identified not only with imposition of an English prayer book but also with what began in 1553 as Forty-Two Articles, reduced in 1553 to Thirty-Nine. These became the doctrinal and liturgical standards for participation in the Anglican Church.

But uniformity was not established without a struggle. The separation of the English Church from Rome was hardly secure. Papal authority, which had been repudiated under Henry VIII and Edward VI, was restored in 1554 under Mary, then repudiated again under Elizabeth. In 1559, Elizabeth was declared "Supreme Governor" of the English Church. The Elizabethan settlement set an "inclusive" tone for Anglicanism in that it did not clearly establish a single variety of Protestant theology, opting instead for imposition of the *Book of Common Prayer* and the theologically hybrid Thirty-Nine Articles. It would later be suggested that the liturgy of the Prayer Book was Roman and the theology of the Articles Calvinist, but, as we will see later, F.D. Maurice strongly objected to this characterization. This settlement marked the reestablishment of the first of the three parties described above, but it did not eliminate the other two. The Elizabethan settlement was threatened on one side by those loyal to Rome and on the other side by a Protestant party that had become distinctly Calvinist in exile under Mary.

The development of English Protestantism in exile under Mary is crucial for two reasons. First, under Calvinist influence, this party turned toward Presbyterian polity. Second, it established connections with Holland that would later prove decisive for development of Baptist, Congregational, and Unitarian denominations in England. The Protestant party that emerged out of exile came to be known as "Puritan" because of its intense commitment to purification of the Church of England. This party understood "purification" as a requirement to purge the English Church of all ceremony and doctrine that did not strictly conform to Scripture, read through Calvinist eyes.

These developments are paralleled and complicated by events in Scotland, where the Reformation took a more decidedly Calvinist turn from the beginning. In Scotland, as in England, political and theological developments were shaped by a balancing act that involved Catholicism, a variety of Protestantisms, and questions of national sovereignty. Scotland allied itself with France as a way to avoid English domination. Then, under the guidance of John Knox, Scotland formed an alliance with England as a way to avoid the domination of Rome.

Knox's theology, formed in Geneva, was unequivocally Calvinist. His politics, formed on a tight wire between England and France, were pragmatic. At a time when Scotland seemed on the verge of becoming a French province, he engineered English involvement that resulted (in 1560) in withdrawal of French troops from Scotland but did not sacrifice Scottish sovereignty. In August 1560, a Calvinist confession drafted by Knox was adopted as a national creed. The first Scottish General Assembly met in December of that same year, and the first *Book of Discipline* was adopted in January 1561. The effect of all this was to establish Presbyterian polity in the Scottish Church, effectively transplanting Calvin's Genevan theocracy to Scotland.

As in England, uniformity was not established without a struggle. Mary (Queen of Scots) returned as a practicing Catholic to Calvinist Scotland in 1561 after the death of her husband (Francis II of France). She remarried and had a son, James VI of Scotland (who later also became James I of England). To make a long story short, she abdicated in 1567, leaving the throne to James (who was a year old at the time). Protestantism was established, in Calvinist and Presbyterian form, by the Scottish Parliament in 1567, and the young king received a Calvinist education.

The development of Calvinism in England proceeded at this time within the confines of the established Anglican Church. During the 1570s, the Puritans undertook Presbyterian experiments within the established structure; but a Separatist party also developed, impatient with waiting for gradual reform. Arguments were developing on several fronts. One involved the dispute over polity. The Puritans argued against episcopacy on the basis of a Calvinist reading of Scripture. Richard Hooker responded by arguing that, while the episcopacy was consistent with Scripture, it was supportable primarily on the basis of its reasonableness.

Hooker's repudiation of Biblicism is an important development in English Church history, but his "reasonableness" was matched by continuing commitment to uniformity that led to a 1593 act of Parliament imposing banishment on those who challenged the sovereign's ecclesiastical authority, refused to go to church, or insisted on worshiping outside established congregations. Resulting exiles, like the ones under Mary, had a profound impact on the development of Protestantisms in England.

In 1603, James VI of Scotland succeeded Elizabeth and became James I of England. Catholics looked to him with hope because of his parentage, Presbyterians because of his education, Anglicans because of his commitment to divine right. Shortly after he became king, he called together a conference of Puritans and Bishops at Hampton Court in January 1604. The only "Puritan" outcome of this conference was the authorized "King James" translation of the Bible into English. The Puritan exodus continued as the established church continued to seek uniformity.

Particularly as a result of Puritan exile in Holland, some segments of English Protestantism came under Arminian influence. Arminianism, which developed out of the teachings of Jacobus Arminius (1560-1609) maintained, in opposition to Calvin, that Christ died not only for the elect but for all humankind. This position emphasized freedom of human choice and was often associated with adult baptism (on the assumption that children were not yet capable of free or conscious choice). Two Separatist leaders who were theologically Arminian, Thomas Helwys and John Murton, established the first permanent Baptist congregation in England in 1611-1612. Another group of Puritans, under the leadership of Henry Jacob, William Ames, and William Bradshaw, outlined an Independent, non-Separatist Congregational position; Jacob founded a Congregational Church in Southwark in 1616. When some members of that congregation left over the question of infant baptism, they established a second Baptist tradition. Those who belong to the first, Arminian, group are known as "General" Baptists, while those who belong to the second, Calvinist, group are known as "Particular" Baptists.

Also as a result of exile in Holland, some segments of English Protestantism came under Socinian influence. Fausto Sozzini (1539-1604), also known as Socinus, emphasized reason and Scripture. Scripture interpreted by human reason was the sole basis on which to judge doctrine and ceremony. He is probably better known for the fact that, on this basis, he rejected the doctrine of the Trinity as unreasonable and unscriptural. This Socinian influence is pivotal in Frederick Maurice's account of the dissenting movement.

The drive toward uniformity continued under James's successor, Charles I, who insisted that subscribers to the Thirty-Nine Articles take them in their literal grammatical sense and imposed an Anglican liturgy on Scotland. The declaration regarding the Thirty-Nine Articles accelerated Puritan exile, while the imposition of an Anglican liturgy in Scotland resulted in open rebellion.

Charles, who had dissolved Parliament in 1629, was forced to call it back into session to finance a war against Scotland. The largely Puritan Parliament was quickly dissolved, Scotland invaded England, and a new Parliament was called, even more Puritan and Presbyterian than the first. This "Long Parliament" imprisoned Archbishop Laud and abolished the High Commission by which ecclesiastical uniformity had been enforced since Henry VIII. Civil War broke out in January 1642, and forces loyal to Parliament (under the command of Oliver Cromwell) defeated the royal army in 1645.

In 1643, while the Civil War was being fought, Parliament abolished the episcopacy and called together the Westminster Assembly, which recommended a Presbyterian system of church government, established in 1646-1647. The Assembly also drafted the Westminster Confession late in 1646. This confession was adopted by the Scottish General Assembly in August 1647 and approved by the English Parliament in June 1648. While full implementation of

Presbyterianism was delayed, Charles intrigued with the impatient Scots (managing to convince them that he would fully establish Presbyterianism) and precipitated another Scottish invasion. Forces under Cromwell's command defeated the invading Scottish army in August 1648. Presbyterians were then expelled from Parliament; Charles was beheaded on 30 January 1649; and Cromwell went on to subjugate Ireland (1649) and Scotland (1650).

After Oliver Cromwell's death, the monarchy was restored in 1660 under Charles II. A new Act of Uniformity effectively barred Puritans from the Church in 1662, and English Nonconformity was transformed officially into Dissent. James II made another attempt to reestablish Catholicism when he issued a "Declaration of Indulgence" on 4 April 1687. When he ordered this Indulgence to be read in all churches in April 1688, seven bishops refused. They were put on trial and acquitted. The Dutch prince William of Orange, who had married James's daughter Mary, was invited to invade in opposition to James. His army landed in England on 5 November 1688; James fled to France. William and Mary became, jointly, sovereigns of England in February (Scotland in May) 1689. The Toleration Act of 24 May 1689 assured that anyone who pledged allegiance to the English sovereign; rejected the jurisdiction of the Pope, the mass, transubstantiation, invocation of the Virgin and saints; and subscribed to the doctrinal positions of the Thirty-Nine Articles was granted freedom of worship. This excluded Catholics but made a place (though not an entirely comfortable one) for the English Free Churches, including the Presbyterians, the Congregationalists, and the Baptists. Presbyterianism was legally established in Scotland in 1690, and England and Scotland were united to form Great Britain in 1707.[3]

3. Lines of Dissent

The dissenting movement that Frederick Maurice draws in his grandfather Michael is not a denomination but a loose amalgamation of Presbyterians, Congregationalists, and Baptists formed out of the complicated history condensed into the last few paragraphs. The intensely anti-creedal character of this diverse group in England is hardly surprising. The peaceful coexistence of Calvinist and Arminian strands, though more surprising, is understandable in conjunction with the rejection of all creeds. Arminians and Calvinists could not agree on a confessional statement, but they could agree on a "presbyterian" (or, more properly, congregational) polity that distinguished them from the established "episcopal" church. They could also agree on the primacy of Scripture and the importance of its being accessible to common people, though they could not agree on the place of reason in interpreting it.

The role of reason in interpreting Scripture is a key factor in the crisis described by Frederick. As noted earlier, Socinus rejected the Trinity as contrary to reason and to Scripture. The "regular" Presbyterian in Frederick's account of the dissenting movement who declared himself a Socinian precipitated a crisis because his declaration rejected a central doctrine of Christianity (the Trinity) in a "presbyterian" context that had formed itself by rejecting all creeds. The question was whether Dissenters would continue to define themselves by rejecting all creeds (thereby including Socinians) or exclude Socinians (thereby establishing a creed).

The story so far suggests that F.D. Maurice grew up in a Dissenting household defined by a conviction that people should believe, in his father Michael Maurice's words, "that to which their conscientious convictions led them."[4] Michael Maurice's emphasis was equally on the unity of God and the reason of human beings; both emphases were characteristic of the English Church, and both had a profound influence on his son.

In this regard, we should bear in mind the extent to which English Unitarianism is rooted in rational criticism of received religion. In the seventeenth century, this was centered particularly in Isaac Newton and John Locke, who replaced revelation with reason as the source of certainty and, who, by connecting God with Nature and Nature with reason, shifted attention toward a "rational" knowledge of Nature demonstrated in an ability to control and predict it. Nature and Scripture are parallel revelations, each to be read in the light of reason tested by experience.

But the story of Maurice's family and the English Church is more complicated still.

In the first place, Michael Maurice operated a school that attracted the children of Unitarians, "orthodox" Dissenters, and members of the Church of England, "partly because," as Frederick puts it, "of the known moderation of the man, partly because of the tolerant and indifferent temper of the time, partly because of the difficulty which then existed of obtaining good places for general education...."[5] This in and of itself resulted in a household characterized by considerable diversity of religious opinion. It also exposed F.D. Maurice to an influential model of educational practice from his earliest years.

In the second place, F.D. Maurice's mother, Priscilla, was a major influence in the household, as were his eight sisters, three of whom were older than he, five younger. As it happens, none of the women in the family remained Unitarian. In an autobiographical fragment written in 1866, F.D. Maurice recalls that when his three older sisters abandoned Unitarianism, they were first influenced by Wesley, then became "strong Calvinists." Maurice goes on to describe Calvinism as "the form of belief which was most offensive to Unitarians and to my father" and to note that "it was still more grievous to him that they seemed to cut themselves off entirely from their childhood by undergoing a second baptism, and being connected with a Society of Baptist Dissenters."⁶ This comes clear against the background of English Church history. The particularity of Calvinism runs contrary to the generality of Arminianism with its openness to human reason. Priscilla gradually joined them, and, when her youngest child was born, "would not consent that there should be any baptism till it should be of age to determine for itself."⁷

When the three older sisters left Unitarianism in 1815, Anne (the youngest of the three, at sixteen) wrote a letter to her father on behalf of all three sisters in which she said "We do not think it consistent with the duty we owe to God to attend a Unitarian place of worship" and that they would no longer take communion with their father.⁸ What makes the letter more remarkable is that all three young women were living at home.

The whole family adopted a policy of writing to one another on matters about which they found it difficult to talk and, more importantly, about which they felt a pronounced need for the clarity and precision of written language. This is a loving family dividing religiously along lines that mirrored the whole society in which it was formed, but they stuck together, and they cared so much about words that they took the time to write it down.

This is where Frederick places his description of his father as "a boy puzzled into silence by the conflicting influences round him."⁹ But F.D. Maurice was not puzzled, as his son notes, into "abstinence from words" so much as he was puzzled into writing, as evidenced by the prolific publication record he maintained throughout his life.

Coming out of this context, F.D. Maurice elected to go to Cambridge, where he could matriculate without professing himself an orthodox Anglican. At Oxford at the time he would have had to sign the Thirty-Nine Articles before he could enroll, while at Cambridge the test came before graduation. Unitarian friends urged him to go to Dublin, where no religious test would be applied. He studied law and left without taking a degree, because he still could not publicly embrace Anglican orthodoxy. He practiced journalism for a while and wrote a novel, *Eustace Conway*, that was published in 1834. Around 1829, he had a much discussed change of heart that enabled him to ascribe to the Thirty-Nine Articles, enter Oxford, and, finally, become a priest. That "change of heart" seems to have involved contact with an important Calvinist theologian, Thomas Erskine, and a Millenarian priest, Joseph Stephenson, as well as his Calvinist, Evangelical, and Unitarian family members. Add to this mix the fact of growing up in a village that was mostly Quaker and Unitarian, a governess who was by turns Quaker, Moravian, and Calvinist, and we have a range of religious influences (with the notable exception of Roman Catholicism) that is as thoroughly ecumenical as was possible in nineteenth-century England.

Speaking here of the "heart" instead of the "head" is appropriate. Maurice was much affected by the Romantic movement via Coleridge, Wordsworth, and (less directly) Schlegel. In this he parallels his mother and older sisters though he does not follow them. They turned from the head to the heart under the influence of Evangelical revivalism. Maurice made the turn by way of Coleridge, and in this he is close to developments in Unitarianism reflected in his contemporary James Martineau.

Unitarianism, under the influence of Richard Price and Joseph Priestley, had become an almost purely rational affair. The reaction of the early nineteenth century under the influence of Romanticism inside and outside Unitarianism was to reconnect head and heart.

The lines also involve political battles, which, as has become evident, cannot be disentangled entirely from the religious ones. The Unitarian tradition with which Michael Maurice was associated was connected (particularly via Priestley and Price) with radical politics and support of the American and French Revolutions. Part of what makes F.D. Maurice so fascinating was that he was not a partisan of that radical political tradition. He was, generally, a thoroughly conservative (even bourgeois) Victorian. That renders his lifelong commitment to social justice (including involvement with workers' cooperatives, Christian Socialism, women's suffrage, higher education for women, and the Working Men's College) puzzling. That the Church of England after the Parliamentary Reform Act of 1832 was "the Conservative Party at prayer" is a commonplace, so it is hardly surprising that Maurice's ordination in 1834 has been judged against his radical roots as a distinctly Rightward turn.

Drawing the lines of history together in a person is instructive, a reminder that historical ages are social conventions and that persons are history's carriers. A "Victorian Age," for example, is socially drawn against the grain: the moment of Victoria's birth (1819) becomes the beginning of an "Age" only after she becomes queen (1837). Does the designation reach back in time and transform the two decades lived after the event but before the designation? The same question can be asked of the "Victorian values" so important in the twentieth-century administration of Margaret Thatcher. Whether the answer is yes in every case is debatable, but events and persons transform practices of history backward as well as forward, and it is instructive to examine the persons and events through which histories are variously recounted. Without getting too far ahead of ourselves, suffice it to say that a distinctively "Maurician" approach to the world locates truth in persons understood as finite intersections of infinite lines rather than in a single line that excludes all the rest. The most remarkable thing about "persons" is our ability simultaneously to be distinct and to include everything.

4. Holy Water for Bourgeois Consciences

Frederick Maurice drew a line through his father and his grandfather when he made a history of the English Church in personal and political terms. A shorter account that also passes through F.D. Maurice is Marx's caustic dismissal of Christian Socialism as holy water sprinkled on the burning conscience of the bourgeoisie.

This line of Marx is more fully articulated by Engels in the introduction he wrote for the English translation of *Socialism: Utopian and Scientific*. That short work began as part of a rather ponderous academic debate with Eugen Dühring of the University of Berlin, three chapters of which were extracted and published in French under the title also adopted for the English edition. The introduction traces two lines relevant to this discussion, one a genealogy that gives historical materialism an English pedigree, the other an account of three great battles in the fight of the bourgeoisie against feudalism (itself a moment in the historical development from feudalism through capitalism to socialism by way of bourgeois and proletarian revolutions).

Engels begins his genealogy of historical materialism with Duns Scotus and nominalism, then traces it through Bacon, Hobbes, and Locke, to Hartley and Priestley. Priestley is the obvious point of contact with Maurice, but Maurice defined his own mature position in opposition to Locke, whose influence on late eighteenth-century revolutionary thought is well known. This is a key for understanding the divergence between the socialism of Marx and Engels and the socialism of Maurice. It is also a key in understanding the distinctively English socialism that emerged from the Victorian Age.

In Engels's account, the three great battles in the fight of the bourgeoisie against feudalism were the Protestant Reformation (by which Engels means especially the Lutheran Reformation in Germany), the "Glorious Revolution" in England (which Engels understands as the culmination of Calvinism), and the French Revolution (which, in Engels's account, jettisons religious trappings and secures the political triumph of the bourgeoisie).

The Lutheran Reformation in Germany is a "religious" revolution with at least two "political" consequences. First, it gives rise to a radical reformation (embodied especially in Thomas Müntzer). Second, in the violent repudiation by Luther of that reformation when he fully embraces the princes against the peasants, it gives rise to a creed for absolute monarchy. In England, Calvinism is transmuted into a "political" revolution with distinctly "religious" overtones. English Calvinism produces a creed for the bourgeoisie reflected in the reversal of relationship between bourgeoisie and monarchy as a result of the "Glorious Revolution" and extended in the "American Revolution." These revolutions enshrined the philosophy of Locke as surely as the theology of Calvin. In France, the "political" revolution replaces "religious" trappings with distinctly "economic" consequences. It secures the political triumph of the bourgeoisie and establishes a groundwork for the parallel "economic" revolution first centered in England, then exported to the rest of Europe.

For Engels, historical development is a necessary and an evolutionary process: what is "later" is an advance over what is "earlier," and Capitalism is a step on the way to Socialism. Socialism is scientific to the extent that it discovers necessity in history under the form of laws by which human action is governed. At this point, it is interesting to note the "descriptive" character of nineteenth-century science, embodied in the observational methods of Engels and Marx as well as Darwin. Engels's roots in Locke make him more surely empiricist than materialist, and his faith in necessity takes a teleological form that results in a confluence with Utilitarianism that might help explain the "socialism" of John Stuart Mill. Engels (like Adam Smith and John Stuart Mill) is convinced that an accurate historical account is a description of the end of Nature and an accurate account of human behavior is a description of the end of human nature. That "freedom" is the end of human nature complicates this for Engels and Mill, but both look for laws by which action can be guided toward that end.

The distinctly English socialism that emerged from the Victorian Age is Fabianism, which is far more deterministic than Marxist socialism because of an optimism that, in retrospect, borders on naivete. This is the socialism that, by the beginning of the twentieth century, enabled the confident (and surprisingly uncontroversial) assertion that "we are all socialists now." It is the socialism that, by the middle of the century, laid the foundation for a Welfare State that rested on a broad popular consensus and could depend on support from conservative as well as liberal politicians.

Marx died before Fabianism was born, so he left no one-liners with which to locate it historically. I suspect that he would have admired it grudgingly as another example of the English genius for maintenance of the *status quo*. His dismissive comment about Christian Socialism marked it as reactionary, an attempt to return to feudal institutions. A more serious criticism would place Christian Socialism with Fabianism as a religious foundation for the political ascendency of the bourgeoisie more durable and reliable than Calvinism. A number of interpreters have voiced the plausible suspicion that Christian Socialism was designed to undercut the revolutionary potential of Chartism. The timing is right. If Communism was the specter haunting Europe in 1848, Chartism was its English incarnation.

That movement originated in frustration at the aftermath of the 1832 Parliamentary Reform Act, a typically English nonviolent *coup d'état* that established bourgeois political power in the wake of the French Revolution. Workers were frustrated by the failure of that Act to accomplish anything more than the institutionalization of middle-class power, and began to agitate for political power of their own.

The Charter itself was not so much a revolutionary program as a demand for universal male suffrage. Its beginnings are often traced to the formation of the London Working Men's Association in 1838, but we would be more accurate to root it in northern industrial organizing and Irish resistance to English rule. The emergence of a London organization did make the Charter visible on the national scene and led to two conventions that functioned in some minds as a parallel parliament with broader representation than the "legally" constituted one.

Chartist power was probably at its peak in 1842, when there was serious consideration of a month-long general strike, based on the "Grand National Holiday" first proposed by William Benbow in 1831, that might well have brought the nation's factories to a grinding halt. As it turns out, that moment was allowed to pass, and later risings at Newport and London were largely ineffective.

If Christian Socialism was designed to undercut the revolutionary potential of Chartism, its formation in 1848 is a tribute to English understatement. The movement was already reconstituting itself at that moment in "cooperative" form, and in many cases Christian Socialism simply baptized the shift. But events unfolded rapidly, as Engels notes in the defeats he enumerates in *Socialism: Utopian and Scientific*, beginning with the collapse of Chartism in April 1848 and ending with the victory of Louis Bonaparte in December 1851.

Engels, the Chartists, and the Fabians shared a faith in the working class that led Engels to place them in the vanguard of the revolution, the Chartists to focus on expanding suffrage to include them, and the Fabians to assume that realizing the Chartist goal of expanded suffrage would lead to socialism without revolution. In the first collection of Fabian essays, Sidney Webb offered a singularly optimistic historical assessment in which such expansion was virtually inevitable. As he saw it, expansion of suffrage in England did not depend on working-class agitation so much as the self-interested maneuvering of parties to expand their political base by gradually expanding the franchise. Engels and Marx were as evolutionary as the Fabians: socialism is in the nature of humanity, and evolution impels humanity toward the end of its nature. Marx was more suspicious of dependence on human reason than Engels, and Engels and the Fabians were more thoroughly utilitarian than Marx.

To a large extent, differing assessments of Chartism depended on different understandings of political representation. Marx and Engels believed that the working class best represented the interests of the whole human community; conservatives (including leaders of the English, American, and French revolutions) believed the rising middle class best represented those interests. Maurice and his colleagues in the Christian Socialist movement suspected that neither class as a class represented the interests of the whole. In Maurice's case, this probably explains his growing emphasis on education. Unless the whole is represented in every part, it is not represented at all.

5. Intersecting Genealogies

We now have a number of intersecting genealogies. For Frederick Maurice, the lines relevant to understanding his father's life are defined by a religious struggle that begins in a question of polity transformed into a question of creed, both understood in a tension between "freedom" and "order." His father's development from dissent to orthodoxy parallels the development of the English Church and the English nation: a central authority (bishop and sovereign) ensures a common creed that is not simply arbitrary and enables a disciplined practice of freedom. An undisciplined practice of freedom (exemplified in Unitarianism) or an arbitrary imposition of will (exemplified in Calvinism) undermine central authority and result in disorder that finally diminishes freedom. Marx's dismissal of Christian Socialism assumes just such a picture and is suspicious of its practice because it baptizes the existing state of affairs and effectively douses any reforming fire that might be kindled by consciousness of human suffering. Engels, perhaps surprisingly, agrees with Frederick Maurice: the "political" and "economic" function of "religious" reformations is the establishment and maintenance of order. They disagree on several particulars. Maurice constructs his father's life on a catholic framework. In an identifiably Anglican fashion, he argues that the Anglican Church is more truly catholic than its alternatives. He sees his father's development toward orthodoxy as a realization that Anglican orthodoxy is a religious embodiment of a divinely established political order. This appears to make Maurice's Anglicanism equivalent to Engels's Lutheranism. The question turns on interpretation of Lutheranism as much as Anglicanism. For Engels, Anglicanism is Calvinist; for Maurice, it is Lutheran, and catholic. Maurice and Engels agree at least in principle that the English Church is conservative, that "revolutionary" tradition is rooted in the Unitarianism of Priestley, the empiricism of Locke, and the materialism of Bacon. Maurice draws his father away from those influences, while Engels draws Marx toward them.

Another prominent contemporary, John Stuart Mill, locates Maurice differently in drawing his own life under the influence of Harriet Taylor from an early *laissez-faire* version of political economy toward a version of socialism that looks like Fabianism. In his *Autobiography*, Mill describes Maurice's participation in the London Debating Society, which Mill and others had organized in 1829. Debates typically divided between Utilitarians (politically "radical") and Tories (politically "conservative"), but Maurice articulated a

Coleridgean alternative to both. This is in substantial agreement with F.D. Maurice's own account in his dedication to the second edition of *The Kingdom of Christ*, where he systematically traces Coleridge's influence on his thought. Because that influence sheds considerable light not only on Maurice but also on socialism's turn under empiricist and utilitarian influence, I will examine it in detail in the next chapter. Suffice it to say for now that Maurice encountered in Coleridge's books a record of his passage through the struggles of his age and, therefore, a guide for readers engaged in the struggles of their own.

Coleridge was a point of entry into an English tradition distinct from the one described by Engels, not simply an "idealist" alternative to Lockean empiricism, but a social alternative to the individualism of both the Utilitarians and Locke, an alternative that insisted on a whole that transcended the sum of individual experiences, in which the "local" was not simply swallowed by the "universal." Maurice locates that insistence in Coleridge's political and theological writings after the French Revolution. This suggests, more than a Kantian heritage shared with Marx, a creative dialectical alternative to Hegelian System. Maurice's development of that method is most explicit in *The Kingdom of Christ*, where he freely acknowledges his debt to Coleridge.

The line through Coleridge to Plato is closely related to and clearly influenced by Cambridge Platonism. Maurice's place in that line is secure even without Coleridge, since he was a student of the great Platonist Julius Hare at Cambridge and continued in close association with him afterward. Though Maurice finally took his degree at Oxford, the spirit of Cambridge Platonism animated his thought, and in Coleridge as much as in Hare he encountered a kindred spirit. While John Stuart Mill insisted that one was born either Platonist or Aristotelian, Maurice maintained that everyone was born Platonist and turned Aristotelian in school. Obviously, the distinction is overdrawn, but its value resides in a recognition shared by both thinkers that whether one's perspective slants toward experience or toward ideas matters. Mills's gradual shift toward socialism, not surprisingly, is additive, while Maurice's embrace of socialism is deductive. The distinction is critical not only in determining the extent to which ideas matter, but also in determining how matter and ideas are embodied in human existence. Because Mill's society is built up out of individuals and experiences, it is nothing and nowhere other than the end. In that sense, it is thoroughly utopian. Maurice's society is the matrix within which individuals and experiences are formed, and it is as present in the beginning and the middle as in the end.

6. Historical Boundaries, Historical Fictions

Frederick's decision to begin his father's biography with his grandfather's life is an intriguing reminder of the fuzziness of historical boundaries. In thinking about F.D. Maurice, Frederick is quite right to begin not with the nineteenth century in which his father was born but with the eighteenth-century events, forces, and people that formed the world he was given. The same may be said of the "Victorian Age," which begins not with Victoria's birth in 1819 or her coronation in 1837 but in the century before. We could keep backing up in infinite regress. But the point is to describe a range that commands our primary attention and to look for developmental patterns in the locations of persons and events. Maurice's comment on Coleridge's books is instructive: he found in them a record of the author's passage through the struggles of his age, a guide for readers passing through the struggles of the next. Here is a broad hint of the philosophical disagreement with Lockean empiricism: we begin not in the beginning but in the middle. The curve of a life is traced from the lives before it into the lives that follow. Here is no blank slate or isolated individual. Our field of vision when we look at F.D. Maurice, who was born in 1805 and died in 1872, must reach from the generation before (1750, shall we say?) through the generation after (1950), recognizing that neither limit is absolute. That two-hundred-year period is equally appropriate for the Victorian Age, recognizing its rootedness in an earlier time and its legacy to a later one. Margaret Thatcher's evocation of the Age suggests a longer reach; but that is a reminder of the flexibility of boundaries at both ends.

Most accounts of the generation before focus on three events: the Industrial Revolution, the "American" Revolution, and the French Revolution. Sometimes, the first of these is described as "economic," while the other two are described as "political." I think it more accurate to look for political and economic dimensions in all three. Recalling Engels's account, we would be more accurate to add a "religious" or "ideological" dimension. Maurice examined all three theologically, and I will have more to say about that in a moment.

Engels described historical development as a movement away from religion through politics toward economics. He reached back beyond the rough edges we have established for our inquiry (1750-1950) to describe a sequence that began with the Protestant Reformation; continued through the "Glorious Revolution" in England, the American and French Revolutions, and the Industrial Revolution; and pointed toward a "proletarian" revolution yet to come. Reading backwards, Lenin could complete the sequence by identifying the Bolshevik Revolution in Russia as the proletarian revolution Engels anticipated. Mao could subdivide the proletarian revolution and argue that one or more of the revolutions in China completed it (though he tended toward the more complicated argument that this "final" revolution must be continuous). The "velvet" revolutions of 1989 can also be incorporated into this sequence from perspectives sympathetic or hostile to Marxist theory. For now, what is most relevant to this discussion is Engels's description of events leading up to the nineteenth century as a transformation in three dimensions: politically, the power of the bourgeoisie is consolidated; economically, feudalism is replaced by Capitalism; religiously, Catholicism is replaced by Calvinism.

Focusing on the English context within which Maurice lived, Engels's account directs our attention to parliamentary reform that culminated in the 1832 Act that effectively established a parliament broadly representative of the bourgeoisie. This describes a curve that is also characteristic of Sidney Webb's later Fabian account that reaches back from 1832 through the Glorious Revolution to the Magna Carta and forward from 1832 through the Chartist Movement and a series of Acts that gradually expanded the franchise. Politically, the English revolutions of the eighteenth and early nineteenth centuries were "peaceful" in that most of the actual fighting took place on foreign soil ("America" and "the Continent"). This is consistent with Edmund Burke's generally reactive account in which British parliamentary reform adopts "American" theories of representation (which were, after all, British in their origins) to undercut the excesses of the French Revolution. Burke supported the American Revolution as consistent with British political theory and reacted to the French Revolution as a cautionary tale.

The "political" question is one of representation. In the American revolution, this escalated from a heated discussion of "virtual" representation into armed rebellion. Oddly enough, however, the political structures devised for the United States were as "virtually" representative as those in Britain. The political question of the eighteenth century, carried over into the nineteenth, was who represents whom. This question carried over from the nineteenth into the twentieth century, as evinced by democratic revolutions that understood representation in terms of Lenin's revolutionary vanguard.

Both Burke and the Fabians insisted on an organic development which has much in common with Coleridge and Maurice. One of the reasons a revolutionary theorist like Thomas Paine (or Richard Price) posed such a threat to Burke is their direct confrontation with this organic approach. Paine was the quintessential rationalist who believed in the power of human reason to accurately identify the distortions and defects of a political system, dismantle it, and rebuild it. Broadly, this is a contrast between the State as organism and the State as machine. This contrast is complicated by a distinction common to Paine, Coleridge, and Maurice between "society" and "government." Their various uses of that distinction are critical to understanding their attitudes toward democracy. In Engels's account, the political revolutions of the eighteenth and early nineteenth centuries agreed that the bourgeoisie best represented the people as a whole, but the revolutions disagreed on how to institutionalize that representation.

With regard to Maurice's Victorian life, we must underscore the extent to which nineteenth-century political reform was connected with educational reform. In England, an expanding franchise developed in tandem with expanding compulsory public education (both of which drove factory reform). The assumption was much like the Jeffersonian insistence that the key to democracy is an educated populace. But here is an interpretive question on which a good deal of political, historical, and pedagogical argument pivots: what is compulsory public (or "common") education for?

In the English tradition (which includes the United States), public education has often started from the assumption that the bourgeoisie best represents the people as a whole and taken the form of a mechanism for enlarging that class. The point has been to "raise" the lower classes, to make the working class middle class. That ninety-eight per cent of the population of the United States identifies itself as "middle class" suggests that (politically, at least) this system has been remarkably effective here. I will return to this later when I consider Maurice's work in adult education. When Maurice turned in 1854 from Christian Socialism to the Working Men's College, he did not abandon politics; and when, in 1848, he joined in establishing both the Christian Socialist movement and Queen's College, he was not working on two separate tracks. Here is another pivot for an argument: if we grant that Maurice was involved in politics at each of these points, was it in fact "politics for the people"?

Economically, Engels's account directs our attention to the rise of the factory system in Britain. The transition from feudalism to capitalism is a "socialization" and a commodification of production. The period described by the rough outlines I defined for this inquiry is marked by centralization of production, transformation of rural into urban society, and a dramatic increase in population. An expanding population concentrated into a limited number of urban areas gave rise to some of the most striking problems on which the attention of Victorian reformers (including Maurice) was riveted.

How these trends are related is the subject of some debate. Increasing population, for example, may be the result of advances in public hygiene, though the resulting urban concentration often worked against those advances. The shape of a city like London in the Victorian Age reflects this tension: an explosion in urban population is followed by a mass exodus of the more affluent toward the edge of the city and beyond, leaving the poorest of the poor in the center. Services and infrastructure follow the affluent. Obviously, the city expands geographically, transforming "rural" into "urban" areas, and population density remains greatest at the center. But the "center" expands in tandem with the "periphery," so the center is viewed with alarm as a growing problem. The solution of choice, moving from the center to the periphery, fuels the process.

At the beginning of this period, individual production was primarily for purposes of individual consumption; only in a limited sense were products transformed into commodities for trade. With the advent of the industrial revolution, mechanical means of production were devised that made it possible for individual workers to efficiently produce more than they needed for personal consumption. Because ownership of these mechanical means of production was limited, some workers began to sell their labor to owners of the means of production and buy what they needed for consumption with the proceeds. Because workers increasingly were separated from the means of production, the products of their labor increasingly became commodities for trade rather than goods for consumption. Either commodities for trade or money for exchange became essential elements of survival. Workers could not produce what they needed for consumption, and the only "commodity" they had for trade was their labor.

From the perspective of owners, accumulation of wealth was dependent on the difference between what they paid their workers (plus the cost of their machinery and its maintenance) and the exchange value of what their workers produced. Not surprisingly, this translated into pressure to produce as much as possible with as few workers as possible and to maximize the exchange value of products while minimizing the wages of their producers. This resulted in long hours, low wages, and unemployment, conditions that are well-documented in the Victorian period.

From the perspective of workers, accumulation of wealth was dependent on the difference between what they paid for subsistence and the wages they were actually paid for their labor. This translated into pressure for higher wages, longer hours, or both. At the extreme, the temptation was to work oneself to death.

From Engels's perspective, the interests of workers and owners are necessarily in conflict, and the conflict results in pressure toward formation of two competing classes. This is why traditional Marxist theory sees capitalism as a necessary and positive step on the way to socialism: it provides the impetus for organization of workers who otherwise would remain unorganized.

A simple minded Utilitarian emphasis on self-interest as the only motivation for human action combined with naive faith that "rational" and unrestrained pursuit by every individual of individual self-interest would result in a "rational" whole serving the interest of every individual led to the thoroughly documented horrors of *laissez-faire* capitalism in the early Victorian Age. Documentation of those horrors laid the groundwork for socialisms such as that of John Stuart Mill and the Fabians. The consensus was that unrestrained pursuit of self-interest in an economic system where workers had been transformed into commodities would increase the misery of the workers. There was a moral dimension to reform movements that emerged in reaction to the condition of factory workers and the urban poor, and I will have occasion to return to this in discussion of the emergence of the Welfare State. That moral dimension, however, paralleled a more strictly "economic" dimension that saw workers as valuable commodities whose destruction was contrary to the self-interest of owners. The problem in this view was not so much increasing misery as decreasing productivity. This, too, demands further discussion. It is the basis for an ameliorative socialism in the service of capitalism and could explain why "socialist" parties in Western Europe so readily worked in the twentieth century within Capitalist economic structures.

The earliest opposition to *laissez-faire* capitalism, epitomized by Carlyle, was reactionary, and, as Engels and Marx suspected, was motivated more by fear of disorder and nostalgia for feudal institutions than by concern for human freedom. That Engels and Marx identified the Christian Socialism with which Maurice was associated and this feudal nostalgia of Carlyle is instructive.

Carlyle and Maurice were repulsed by the idea of a society grounded on competition. Maurice made that repulsion the basis for his definition of socialism, which had more to do with cooperation than with public ownership of the means of production. In examining Maurice's thought, I will return to this question: how did he distinguish himself from the reactionary romanticism of Carlyle?

Recall that Mill identified Maurice's approach as a Coleridgean "third way" distinct from both Carlyle and Utilitarianism. Philosophically and politically, the difference is one of direction. Carlyle looked back when he looked for "society." Mill looked forward. For Carlyle, the problem was how to recover society. For Mill, the problem was how to make it. But for Coleridge, particularly in Maurice's reading, the problem was how to realize it. The distinctions are subtle but crucial, especially when viewed through Maurice's theological lens.

To put the matter briefly: Engels saw the Anglican Church as Calvinist; if Maurice had seen it as such, he would not have joined. The reason is that Maurice located the center of Calvinism in will, while he located the center of Christianity in incarnation.

Maurice would have no problem with Engels's characterization of Calvinism as a creed for the bourgeoisie. His only problem with characterization of Lutheranism as a creed for absolute monarchy would be with the term "absolute."

Maurice's identification with monarchy is as problematic as Luther's identification with the princes. Both were playing a dangerous political game intended to avoid absolutism. Whether either succeeded is doubtful, but, if the absolute monarchs that followed the Reformation are admissible as evidence against Luther, then Stalin may be cited as evidence against Engels. Absolutism is a difficult political and philosophical problem, and Maurice was thoroughly Lutheran in his conviction that will would exacerbate it rather than solve it. His attempt to work out the political and philosophical implications of that theological conviction is a record of his passage through the struggles of his age. To repeat it would be foolish and irrelevant. To use it as a guide in engaging the struggles of our age, however, has promise.

That "the Victorian Age" is a hotly contested historical fiction as well as a useful heuristic device poses relevant questions for discussion of F.D. Maurice's "Victorian" life. "The Victorian Age" is heuristically useful not so much because of its contribution to historical periodization (that is a large part of what makes it a contested fiction), but because of what it tells us about the people and processes that construct it.

The term itself was coined in 1851, fourteen years into Victoria's sixty-four year reign. In retrospect, the "Age" marks a time in which England particularly (and Great Britain generally) was transformed from an agricultural economy based on domestic production by an overwhelmingly rural population to an industrial economy based on a factory system that could not exist apart from an overwhelmingly urban population. Considerable debate arises over whether the economic transformation from domestic production to factory system was a revolution or an evolution, but its concentration on a small island in the nineteenth century certainly had revolutionary potential when combined with expanding population and urbanization on an historically unprecedented scale.

The social and political transformation from country to city was central to Victorian self-understanding and therefore to Maurice's theological exploration of social questions. His discussion of society takes place against a background of urbanization that profoundly affects the way people think about themselves and each other, whether or not they themselves migrate from country to city. When Maurice asks after "the Kingdom of Christ," he asks a question that is very much on the mind of his contemporaries: what is the shape of God's realm, and how is it related to the necessarily human realms in which we live? As a parallel process to drawing historical lines through persons, Maurice and his contemporaries proposed drawing historical lines through nations.

This is related to the earlier discussion of "representation," and it is a continuation of the long dispute over sovereignty that has marked European history. In European thought, "people" and "nation" as concepts were formed in controversy regarding representation and sovereignty; the controversy and the formation of the concepts can be traced in domestic and international developments from the eighteenth into the twentieth century.

In one of the more intriguing metaphorical descriptions of the Victorian Age, Asa Briggs locates it not between the French Revolution and the twentieth century but between the arrival of the railroad and the advent of the automobile. That metaphor demands attention to the shape of the city as well as the shape of the kingdom. Both shapes are familiar topics for Christian theological reflection, particularly in the Augustinian tradition that includes Maurice. For inhabitants of nineteenth century Great Britain, the shapes are not easy to distinguish: city in general and London in particular define the kingdom. In this regard, too, Maurice is representative. His theological reflection emerges against the background of a move to London that parallels at least one version of the movement of the century.

Diversity of opinion exists regarding the movement of the century. Is our attention focused on the transition from "rural" to "urban" or from "domestic production" to "factory system"? Do we resolve the tension of the century in favor of "North" or "South," "new cities" or "old," "provincial" or "metropolitan"? As is clear from the sociological literature that emerged at the end of the period, we must also attend to which side of London occupies an observer's attention (and, for many contemporary voices, which side of London the observer occupies).

Briggs's metaphor suggests a movement from the "collective" dimension of railroads toward the "private" dimension of automobiles as determining factors in the shape of cities, from the social toward the individual. This is striking since most socialist literature in English (from Robert Owen through Michael Harrington) has agreed that the rise of capitalism coincides with the socialization of production. Two contradictory trends are at work: "modern" cities embody the human concentrations necessary for the factory system, yet they are increasingly shaped by automobiles which symbolize the triumph of individualism.

Maurice died before automobiles began to shape cities, but much of his writing was a response to the tension between individuation and socialization characteristic of the age in which he wrote. He spoke not only from his experience of migration to London but also in response to his experience of the displaced persons who occupied it as a result of the urbanization of the nineteenth century. When he looked at Chartist demonstrators in London in 1848, he saw individuals looking for society, individuals lost in a city where they saw nothing but wilderness. In good Augustinian fashion, the city became the question.

7. Three Revolutions

Three revolutions from the end of the seventeenth century to the end of the eighteenth give rise to three dominant strands of political philosophy at the beginning of the Victorian Age.

At the end of the seventeenth century, John Locke articulates the outcome of the Glorious Revolution in two areas crucial for subsequent political philosophy: private property and public sovereignty. In Locke, both are derived from Nature by human action. In the State of Nature, property is common; it is made private by human work. Private property is Nature that has been transformed by human labor. This is one source of the labor theory of value common to socialist thought and Political Economy. Sovereignty, too, is common (or general) in the State of Nature; it is made particular by the human institution and practice of civil society. The sovereignty of the crown is doubly derivative, a particular sovereignty granted in civil society instituted from Nature. The immediate backdrop for Locke's philosophy is the beginning of enclosure, which transforms common property into private property, and the monarchy of William and Mary instituted in the Revolution directly by Parliament's action, only indirectly by God's.

Near the end of the eighteenth century, Jeremy Bentham articulates a revolution in progress. Like the Industrial Revolution, Bentham's philosophy diminishes Nature by transforming it into civil society. At its extreme, it reduces Nature to the utilitarian principle of happiness and expands civil society to include every instance of its implementation by human action. Because this philosophy develops in tandem with the American and French Revolutions, it effectively replaces the derivative sovereignty of the crown with popular sovereignty in one of two forms: particular or general. As it develops into Political Economy, Bentham's philosophy characteristically identifies "particular" popular sovereignty with the individual's pursuit of happiness and "general" popular sovereignty with the sum total of all individual pursuits of happiness. This effectively conflates "general" popular sovereignty with Adam Smith's invisible hand and brings the question of "particular" popular sovereignty to the forefront. This is consistent with an axiological turn in British thought embodied in economic, ethical, and psychological forms. The question of sovereignty is addressed with reference to human action, which connects sovereignty (or will) with value, and value with the transformation of Nature.

At the beginning of the nineteenth century, Samuel Taylor Coleridge articulates another revolution more generally understood as reaction. By reasserting Nature, Coleridge sets out to transform civil society, which, in the Industrial and French Revolutions, has taken a decidedly uncivil turn. Because Coleridge first embraces both Bentham and the French Revolution, his attention is subsequently riveted on the distortion of Nature by assertion of human will. Whereas Bentham's philosophy equates that assertion, guided by pursuit of happiness, with reason, Coleridge's philosophy identifies it with the irrational destruction of Nature. Sovereignty is still in question, and it is still addressed with reference to human action, but "popular" sovereignty in its "particular" form requires moderation. Unmoderated, it is not reason at all, but irrationality.

The axiological turn in Coleridge digs into rationality and seeks to reconfigure the relationship between Nature and civil society. In his attention to roots, Coleridge represents the most radical of the three philosophical strands.

When Max Beer wrote his *History of British Socialism* at the beginning of the twentieth century, he found Roman, particularly Stoic, roots. These roots form the background against which the political philosophies of Locke, Bentham, and Coleridge emerged.

A Stoic distrust of property was baptized early and rooted on British soil, along with a Roman distinction between "natural" and "civil" law. The Christian form of this distinction is an account of the Fall in which eviction from Paradise coincides with the beginning of work, and eviction from the land coincides with the beginning of cities. People who live in cities live in perpetual exile from the land. Natural law's superiority to civil law is that of a Platonic ideal. Never realized, it is always present and always regulative.

This Platonic/Stoic/Christian line of thought is taken up in monasticism and developed most fully with the emergence of the preaching orders in the thirteenth and fourteenth centuries at the same time that they are forming the "ancient" universities, which in England means Oxford and Cambridge.

The Franciscan Order in particular takes the fallenness of property to heart and advocates absolute poverty. This is a political claim that directly confronts civil authority, derived from the Fall. In Franciscan history, the question of poverty led to a break between radicals and moderates in which the moderates ultimately determined the shape of the Order. British thinkers were in the vanguard of both developments: Duns Scotus represented the moderate position, while William of Ockham represented the radical one. In this controversy, the moderate position accepted common property as consistent with Nature, while the radical position rejected property altogether.

In Beer's genealogy, both wings of Franciscan thought are conduits through which Isidore's distrust of property feeds socialism. Dominican thought, embodied in Thomas Aquinas, takes up the "naturalization" of property by the Franciscan Alexander of Hales and lays the foundation for capitalism.

Ockham's most notable English disciple is John Wycliffe, whose spirit infused the Reformation in England. As Beer notes in passing, F.D. Maurice is a spiritual descendent of Wycliffe by way of Coleridge. That is decisive for Maurice's theology as well as for his contribution to political philosophy.

Ockham describes three moral stages in human history: *ante lapsum* (before the Fall, characterized by natural equity and the absence of property), *post lapsum* (after the Fall, characterized by the imposition of Reason and Law), and corruption (characterized by private property and civil dominion). The sequence is usually read as a descriptive philosophy of history, but this leads to misunderstanding.

The process, as Coleridge and Maurice were aware, calls for an archeological rather than a sequential reading. The whole process as described by Ockham is a Fall from grace. Locating the Fall between the first and second stages leads to a reactionary philosophy of history like Carlyle's or Southey's (and, surprisingly, like Godwin's or Paine's). In this reading, *laissez-faire* is the lowest circle of hell. Civil dominion, Reason, and Law are at best stop-gap mechanisms by which to drag humanity back from the corruption into which it has fallen to the state of grace from which it began. At worst, they are permanent structures that condemn humanity to the limbo between grace and corruption. Locating the Fall in the whole process leads to a more complex understanding of time in which one must constantly dig below the surface corruption to reach the always present depth of grace.

Maurice was dismissed from his teaching position at King's College because of his attention to this concept of time in his *Theological Essays*, which those who dismissed him rightly recognized as being of a piece with his political activity as a leader of the Christian Socialist movement. Development of this concept of time was the most revolutionary political action that Maurice undertook, and in this development he most fully realized Ockham's legacy via Coleridge. Luther's most revolutionary insights, that the Christian is simultaneously saint and sinner, simultaneously bound and free, derive from Ockham. What passes as political (and economic) realism assumes that we are neither saints nor sinners and sets about busily to construct mechanisms with which to sustain our suspension between the two states and to delude us into believing that such suspension is freedom. Ockham's revolutionary legacy to Luther and Maurice reveals the suspension as a temptation that permanently separates us not from sin but from grace. Maurice's offense in *Theological Essays* was to clearly articulate a philosophy of time that identified such separation as the presence of hell.

In a sense, every post-Wycliffe English thinker (and every post-Luther German thinker) is a spiritual descendent of Ockham. Much of the discussion in political philosophy from the English Reformation through the nineteenth century can be recast in these terms, with a running dispute regarding the time of transition from the "natural" to the "civil" state and the proper relationship between the two. A common reading (consistent with the one adopted by Engels and Marx) concentrates on the dissolution of feudalism, which poses two problems with moral, political, and economic dimensions: constitution of a central, national authority to replace decentralized feudal authority and protection of the displaced and powerless peasantry. In this, Locke reverses Wycliffe. While Wycliffe sanctioned personal monarchy and defended communal ownership of land, Locke condemns personal monarchy and sanctions private property. Maurice (along with Luther and Coleridge) is more like Wycliffe in this regard than Locke. Locke looked to popular sovereignty as a limit on the destructive potential of personal monarchy and saw private property as protection against the arbitrary appropriation of free human labor. Maurice looked to personal monarchy as a limit on the destructive potential of popular sovereignty, and he saw communal (or cooperative) ownership as a limit on the destructive potential of individual acquisitiveness.

8. Diggers

In this regard, I cannot help thinking that Maurice's insistent description of the theologian as digger was an intentional reference to those true levellers called by that name in the seventeenth century because they literally occupied and cultivated common ground. Beer describes their substantial theoretical base as mystical religion with Reason as its axis that superseded "logical" Scholastic theology. "It was," he writes, "as if all the Peasant Wars of the past had suddenly become articulate."[10] Becoming articulate in this case signifies a turn away from violent revolution but not away from direct action. That turn echoes in Maurice's clear statement some two hundred years later: "Competition is put forth as the law of the universe. That is a lie. The time is come for us to declare that it is a lie by word and deed."[11] One way to protect a displaced peasantry is, with the peasantry, to take place.

Stanley Pierson gestures toward this in his recognition of Anglican and nonconformist visions of a Christian commonwealth fed by three streams of thought in the nineteenth century: social romanticism (Thomas Carlyle and John Ruskin), Utilitarianism (John Stuart Mill and Robert Owen), and Christian (Coleridge, the Tractarians, and Thomas Arnold).

The categories are fuzzier than Pierson implies, though the separation of Coleridge from "social" romanticism may clear up some misunderstandings. Pierson's inclusion of Coleridge, the Tractarians, and Thomas Arnold in the same category is problematic. If anything, Coleridge is closer to Carlyle and Ruskin than to the Tractarians. But Coleridge is in a class by himself, a stream that often crosses the romantic stream or runs parallel to it and feeds Maurice, the Tractarians, and Arnold, as well as Percy and Mary Shelley. Coleridge's influence on socialism is via Maurice; Arnold enters via Ludlow, often in opposition to Maurice and Coleridge. Coleridge's distinctive contribution, taken up by Maurice, is a metaphysical dimension, which Pierson calls an interest in the "deep underground principles of society."[12]

One source of misunderstanding that has plagued both Coleridge and Maurice derives from their conviction that this metaphysical dimension is inextricably bound with the ethical. Where Ludlow and Maurice differed, it was often because Ludlow saw Maurice's metaphysical turn as a diversion from the ethical and political tasks at hand. Readers of Maurice and Coleridge have often interpreted that turn as a retreat from politics precipitated by the horrors of the French Revolution. But it was no such thing. The theologian is a digger, and digging is simultaneously a metaphysical, a political, and an ethical task.

Separate the social-ethical dimensions of Maurice's thought from the metaphysical, and the social-ethical becomes groundless, while the metaphysical becomes static. The Coleridgean contribution is a dynamic ground and a struggle to recover the ideal of an organic commonwealth, both of which are consistent with the hostility to system that pervades Coleridge and Maurice.

Two
A CIRCLE OF FRIENDS

Maurice read Coleridge's writing as a record of his passage through the struggles of his age. *Biographia Literaria* is the midpoint of that record, a midlife condensation constructed on an autobiographical framework that carries two remarkable bursts of philosophical speculation (each with the promise of more to come) and a sustained critical theory with important literary, political, and theological repercussions.

Though the work was prepared for publication, it has the appearance of a document Coleridge wrote for himself as much as for a public, guided, I suspect, by sentiments committed to writing in the last chapter of the work: that "we are so framed in mind, and even so organized in brain and nerve, that all confusion is painful" and that "we must not only love our neighbors as ourselves, but ourselves likewise as our neighbors."[1] A literary biography, this work has the appearance, too, of a bibliography annotated at length with the life of the poet.

1. A Literary Life

Coleridge constructed this work from the perspective of midlife. Every autobiographical act addresses questions of beginning and ending that have been central to literary criticism since Aristotle. Like any other literary work, the autobiography stands or falls by the way in which its beginning, middle, and end are woven together. By writing from a midlife perspective, Coleridge places all three parts in the middle of his life: how they are woven together forms a beginning and an end outside the work in the world, either of which can be reformed again and again in other constructions. More explicitly than other literary works, an autobiography is the author's construction in writing of his or her own life. In this work, Coleridge constructs his life both as a fragment (the midlife perspective undermines the temptation to view it as finished) and as a whole: the work embodies his dynamic philosophy. He makes his self for himself, and, at the same time, he makes a self for us as he makes us (and we make ourselves) an audience, a public.

Coleridge's first words,

> It has been my lot to have had my name introduced, both in conversation, and in print, more frequently than I find it easy to explain, whether I

consider the fewness, unimportance, and limited circulation of my writings, or the retirement and distance in which I have lived, both from the literary and political world,[2]

give the impression of an author who would prefer to write himself out of the public eye. But these words are not the beginning of the work. The work begins with a hint from Goethe:

> Little call as he may have to instruct others, he wishes nevertheless to open out his heart to such as he either knows or hopes to be of like mind with himself, but who are widely scattered in the world: he wishes to knit anew his connexions with his oldest friends, to continue those recently formed, and to win other friends among the rising generation for the remaining course of his life.[3]

Inexplicably dragged into the eye of an anonymous public, Coleridge writes to weave a circle of friends, to reweave an order of familiarity against confusion.

We have here not a passive record of what Coleridge read, but an active record of Coleridge writing his reading at the same time that he writes his life. This is a kindred spirit for a child puzzled out of speech into silence, into words, and into writing.

Coleridge's autobiographical framework moves on two tracks, from associationism toward transcendental philosophy and from Utilitarianism toward Nationalism. This appears consistent with an account of his life already common by 1817 that couples his philosophical development from materialism to idealism with a political move from Left to Right and a theological move from Dissent to Orthodoxy. These philosophical, theological, and political developments have been associated with his role in the origins of the Romantic movement in English literature, the beginning of which is sometimes located in his publication (with Wordsworth) of *Lyrical Ballads* in 1798. The image with which Coleridge begins suggests that he judged the public characterization of his life as confused, so we are well advised to appropriate it with caution.

That Coleridge describes himself as living in retirement from both political and literary worlds points to the conscious withdrawal described in *Biographia Literaria* and directs our attention to his critical theory as the best source of insight in this document into his politics and his poetry.

His philosophy and theology are illuminated by two bursts of philosophical speculation. The first, beginning in Chapter 5, is a critique of Hartley's associationist theory and a rudimentary outline of a perceptual theory that parallels Goethe's and anticipates twentieth-century developments in ecological psychology. This passage helps in understanding Maurice and the development of socialism because it confronts a divorce of theory from practice already well underway in the nineteenth century that has had a profound political impact in the twentieth. The second burst, beginning in Chapter 12, is an account of transcendental philosophy that serves not only as a record of Kant's entry into English thought but also as an original contribution to what Coleridge calls dynamic philosophy, a neglected alternative to other philosophies of internal relations developing at about the same time in Hegel and, later, in opposition to Hegel among the "young Hegelians" and Marx. This second burst is a corrective to the tendency to read Maurice's socialism through Marxist (or worse, Hegelian) eyes.

The perceptual theory that Coleridge begins to elaborate in Chapter 5 has its origins in a statement near the beginning of the book, "I labored at a solid foundation, on which permanently to ground my opinions, in the component faculties of the human mind itself,"[4] that is a good summary statement of one aspect of Coleridge's philosophical work that clearly affected Maurice. This labor toward a single solid foundation ran in tandem with a movement away from Unitarianism. Like Maurice, Coleridge holds fast to the Unitarian emphasis on unity even as he abandons Unitarianism itself.

Coleridge begins his fifth chapter by describing a class of thinkers who have been "impelled as by an instinct to propose their own nature as a problem."[5] Historically, these thinkers began by categorizing, constructing tables of distinctions on the basis of the presence or absence of will. Sensations, perceptions, movements were separated into three categories: active, passive, or a combination of both. This resulted in a "materialist" understanding of perception identified with Hobbes and Gassendi. The categories were refined by a distinction between the voluntary and the spontaneous that resulted in an "idealist" understanding of perception identified with Berkeley.

Behind this shorthand description is a genealogy that traces materialism and idealism to Presocratic roots and gives them a common origin in the problem of human nature, particularly the nature of human thinking. This is an early hint that Coleridge will collapse epistemological and ontological questions, then look for common ground beneath what appear to be mutually exclusive positions.

2. Common Ground

In this case, the common ground is a more fundamental distinction, that between thoughts and things. With regard to things, causation appeared to be external; with regard to thoughts, causation appeared to be internal. Internal experience was then categorized, just as external experience had been, according to whether it was passive, voluntary, or spontaneous. Spontaneous experience occupied a middle ground between passive and voluntary. Speculation on modes of action led to inquiry regarding laws that govern action. In Egypt, Palestine,

Greece, and India, this speculation did not wait for development of experimental research, so it proceeded under the rubric of philosophy (specifically metaphysics) rather than experimental psychology.

Experimental psychology was emerging at the time Coleridge wrote. He refers to James Mackintosh, who had announced in a series of lectures that the law of association had been established as the basis for experimental psychology, which would henceforth contain metaphysical speculation. Emphasis on containment (in this case containment of philosophical abstraction by scientific experimentation) has led to description of the Victorian Age as a culture of containment, though what (or who) is contained and what (or who) is containing is perpetually contested terrain. Mackintosh credited Thomas Hobbes with discovery of the law of association and David Hartley with its generalization. Hartley, Mackintosh said, stood in the same relation to Hobbes as Newton to Kepler; the law of association stood in the same relation to mind as the law of gravity to matter.

At this point, Coleridge distinguishes himself philosophically from Mackintosh in the strongest possible terms but brackets the philosophical argument regarding whether association's relation to mind is analogous to gravity's relation to matter, turning instead to the historical question regarding discovery of the law of association. On this point, Hobbes was anticipated by Descartes and, Coleridge maintains, did nothing in any case to distinguish a law of association from general laws that govern motion and interaction of material bodies. Descartes built up a theory of language on the basis of association, which, like Hobbes, he interpreted as a mechanistic process. Hobbes made a series of physiological claims based not on the discovery of a law of association but on the assumption that it was already an admitted fact: When a sense is impinged upon by an external object, motion is induced in the sensory organ. This motion produces a representation of the external object, a disposition to repeat the motion. When we perceive several objects simultaneously, all the resulting movements of sensory organs are linked. Subsequently, if any one of the linked movements is induced by perception of an object, all of them are induced mechanically by the link. Coleridge concludes that Hobbes, Hartley, and others who attribute thoughts to the motion of sensory organs induced by external objects and derive association from material connection among these sensory organs reduce the law of association to a law of time. However, because Hobbes allows that an idea represented by stimulation of a sensory organ can be associated with an idea represented by memory, even this temporal law is imprecise.

In a further note on imprecision, Coleridge laments the English usage of "idea" common since Hume. The Greek ἰδέα, he reports, was originally used to indicate the visual representation of a distant object, "when we see the whole without distinguishing its parts." Plato adopted it as a technical term distinguished from εἴδωλα, "the transient and perishable emblems" of ideas. Ἰδέα was seen as mysterious and living, εἴδωλα as a mechanical and transitory operation.[6]

Coleridge traces the law of association to earlier sources than either Hobbes or Descartes, ultimately to Aristotle's *De Anima, De Memoria,* and *Parva Naturalia.* In Aristotle's account, every partial representation may recall any whole representation of which it has been a part. "Whole" representations are composed of ideas that may be associated by any of five causes: (1) connection in time (simultaneity or sequentiality), (2) proximity or connection in space, (3) interdependence or cause and effect, (4) likeness, and (5) contrast. Association, then, is the law that governs passive perception and mechanical memory. Coleridge maintains that later writers, including Hobbes, Hume, and Hartley, do nothing more than repeat Aristotle or, where they differ from him, introduce error or unsubstantiated speculation.

Coleridge attributes materialist explanations such as that of Hartley to a "despotism of the eye" that privileges the visible and seeks to explain what is invisible by transforming it into something accessible to vision. This drives Hartley to "explain" ideas by transforming them into material vibrations of internal sensory organs produced by the action of external objects.

Hartley accounts for association of ideas as follows: an external object A produces an internal vibration a in a sensory organ. A becomes associated with the internal vibration m that results from another external object M when internal vibration a propagates itself by producing internal vibration m. But this requires that two entirely different causes (external object M and internal vibration a) produce the same effect, meaning that they are not entirely different but already mysteriously associated. Coleridge allows that we might argue that the oscillating ether of the nerves in which a and m occur acquires a disposition to their respective vibrations by repeated exposure to objects A and M. Then repeating a would reproduce m, presumably because, given the acquired disposition, the ether in which m occurs will be disposed to produce m or not to vibrate at all. Coleridge is prepared to grant the possibility of such a disposition in a material nerve, but to call it a "disposition" makes as much sense as saying a weather vane in a place where the prevailing wind is easterly has acquired a habit of turning east. We gain nothing from the supposed disposition. The "explanation" of ideas as vibrating nerves is like the stone to which the unsuspecting villagers in the old story add vegetables, water, and seasoning to make a delicious stone soup.

Priestley, Coleridge reports, edits the vibrating nerves out of Hartley, removing Hartley's material hypothesis. The result is an impoverished version of Aristotle that reduces association to contemporaneity, proximity in space and time. In this account, Coleridge objects, will, reason, judgment, and understanding are made effects rather than causes of association. Our lives are "divided between the despotism of outward impressions, and that of senseless and passive memory."[7] No place exists in this system for comprehension, the active power of imagination.

Coleridge recounts the case of an illiterate German woman in her midtwenties who contracted a fever during which she babbled in Latin, Greek, and Hebrew. Priests and neighbors generally agreed that the young woman was possessed, a conclusion reinforced by the known fact that she had been a heretic. The case attracted the attention of a young physician who was determined to find an explanation for the woman's behavior. He took copious notes and translated the words and phrases she had spoken in her feverish state. Some of the Hebrew was from the Bible, but most was (as Coleridge puts it) in "the rabbinical dialect." He went on to meticulously trace her background until he found the place where she grew up. As it turns out, she was raised from an early age in the household of a pastor who used to walk around the house reading aloud passages from his favorite books, which included rabbinic texts in Hebrew, as well as Christian theological works in Latin and Greek. The young physician was able to trace the woman's words to these sources. Coleridge concludes from this that relics of sensation can remain in a latent state for extended periods, that thoughts may be imperishable. But it also leads him to associate meaning with organization. The feverish young woman retained words and fragments in her memory which were released by the stimulus of her fever, but this passive, mechanical retention did not include comprehension.

This account has no room for soul, except as an ethereal string randomly plucked by the body. This, too, is problematic, because the two substances, body and soul, have no property in common. Hartley's followers, according to Coleridge, abandon the soul altogether as a separate substance and recast it as consciousness "considered as a *result*, as a *tune*, the common product of the breeze and the harp." This leads Coleridge, though, to ask after the tune: what is harmony if not "a mode of relation, the very *esse* of which is *percipi*?" Unless the soul is a rational being that presupposes the power that, by perceiving, creates the tune, he finds this explanation incomprehensible.[8]

Hartley's logic replaces the agent with what Coleridge derisively designates "a *something-nothing-every-thing*, which does all of which we know, and knows nothing of all that itself does."[9] Because the ethical and theological implications of this replacement are unacceptable to Coleridge, he reconsiders the entire system.

The system rests on conflation of the conditions of a thing with its causes and essence, the conflation of processes by which we arrive at knowledge of a faculty with the faculty itself. Having resolved our confusion by properly distinguishing conditions from causes and processes by which we come to know faculties from the faculties themselves, Coleridge cross-examines Hartley's system. Contemporaneity, Coleridge says, is a law of matter that is also a limit or condition of the laws of mind. It is to thought as gravitation is to locomotion. When we walk (or jump), we first counteract gravitation in order subsequently to take advantage of it. A jump consists of an act of resistance to gravity and a submission to it. Without the first, we would not go up; without the second, we would not come down. Coleridge suggests a similar process in the act of thinking, which consists of two powers, one active, one passive, and an intermediate faculty (imagination) that combines both.

Because contemporaneity is a condition for all association, it is present in every instance of association. This constant presence could lead an observer to conclude that contemporaneity is the substance, essence, or cause of association. This would be like concluding that air is the substance, essence, or cause of our lives because it is present as a condition whenever or wherever we are alive. Without it we would die; but that it is the cause of our lives does not follow. Coleridge gives the example of an associative chain in which a person who has eaten fish with gooseberry sauce thinks of gooseberries upon seeing a fish. Thinking of gooseberries, the person thinks of a goose; thinking of a goose brings a swan to mind even though the person has never seen the two birds together. This movement in thought from fish to swan is not adequately explained by proximities in time, though such proximities are active in every link of the chain. This leads Coleridge to restate the law of association:

> whatever makes certain parts of a total impression more vivid or distinct than the rest, will determine the mind to recall these in preference to others equally linked together by the common condition of contemporaneity, or (what I deem a more appropriate and philosophical term) of *continuity*.[10]

Continuity, then, is a condition of association, but attention determines which associations in a potentially infinite array are activated.

The potentially infinite array of associations raises a question that concerned Leibniz. By connecting thought with things, the array of associations effectively undermines the absolute distinction between mind and matter introduced by Descartes. To the extent that associative chains such as the one described by Coleridge exist, they may be taken as evidence of matter's action on mind and provide a basis on which to contend that mind and matter are two modes of a common substance rather than entirely separate substances. Leibniz seized this possibility as the basis for his pre-established harmony. Some of his followers seized it as a basis for hylozoism, which maintains that every body down to the smallest atom has a soul.

Coleridge dismisses pre-established harmony and hylozoism at the same time that he dismisses materialism. Matter, he says, has no inward, but the inward is of most significance. Material associative explanations may account for surface interactions that have no depth. But we encounter objects and depths in our perceptions: "It is the object itself, not the product of a syllogism, which is present to our consciousness."[11]

This is an interesting reversal. The materialist hypothesis reduces perception to encounters with phantoms that emerge from chains of mechanical association. But Coleridge the idealist is not satisfied with phantom encounters. We perceive objects, not ghosts.

Materialism as it has been taught is unintelligible. When it becomes intelligible, it ceases to be materialism.

Coleridge promises to elaborate in a future work, which, as it turns out, he never delivered. He describes the work as a commentary on the Gospel of John that develops the idea of a human and divine productive logos. We are left with a development of the idea in three points contained in a single paragraph at the end of Chapter 8: (1) association presupposes the existence of thoughts and images to be associated; (2) the hypothesis of an external world exactly corresponding to internal images that we actually perceive replaces the immediacy and reality of perception with a phantom world; and (3) the formation of a copy is not explained simply by the existence of an original. As Coleridge puts it, "the copyist of Raphael's Transfiguration must repeat more or less perfectly the process of Raphael."[12] Geometric optics cannot explain an image on the retina, and an image on the retina cannot explain vision or thought. Such an explanation is an only slightly more sophisticated variation on the theme made famous in Bertrand Russell's story of his encounter with a woman who insisted that the world rested on the back of a giant turtle. When he asked her what held up the turtle, she responded, "It's turtles all the way down." No matter how sophisticated our understanding of perceptual mechanisms or optics may become, it is the perceptual process to which we must attend, and that is the direction Coleridge takes in his insistence on imagination as active comprehension.

3. A System of Philosophy

The *Biographia Literaria* does not make a sharp distinction between what I have called two bursts of philosophical speculation. They are joined by an important part of the annotation to which I referred at the beginning of this chapter, a reference to a succession of "schools" through which Coleridge moved: Locke, Berkeley, Leibniz, Hartley. At the end of the succession (described at the beginning of Chapter 9), Coleridge says, he began to ask himself whether "a system of philosophy, as different from mere history and historic classification" is possible.[13]

That question primed him for the philosophy of Kant, but it directed him first through Jakob Böhme, William Law, and George Fox. The succession is intriguing, if incomplete. It includes British empiricists at both ends and a German rationalist in the middle; it moves between idealism and materialism; and it paves the way for Kant by moving through mysticism after expressing dissatisfaction with mere historical description. That the succession is incomplete as a record of Coleridge's reading is evinced by the omission of Descartes, Hobbes, and Hume. Adding them lends credence to Coleridge's claim to have arrived at something like transcendental philosophy even before he encountered Kant.

Coleridge and Kant apparently followed similar routes out of dogmatism through skepticism to transcendentalism. Dissatisfaction with mere historical description is crucial for subsequent developments. Marx was as Kantian as Coleridge when, in his eleventh thesis on Feuerbach, he expressed a desire to move from interpretation toward transformation of the world: reason must be "practical" as well as "pure." That the problematic way between interpretation and transformation must be explored is a critical ethical and political legacy of encounter between British and German thought.

Coleridge's exploration of the territory is a clue to understanding his suspicion—and Maurice's—of democracy, and Coleridge's exploration takes an "idealist" tack opposite to the one later taken by Marx. Hegel had a great deal to do with the turn Marx took. That Hegel was not an influence on Coleridge helps explain the difference in the approaches of Marx and Coleridge.

It is neither possible nor necessary for the masses to be philosophers. Coleridge says that a "philosophic consciousness" lies beneath "spontaneous consciousness." Philosophic consciousness, "actualized by an effort of freedom," is artificial or synthetic, while spontaneous consciousness is "natural to all reflecting beings." Objects of human knowledge may be divided into those on this side of spontaneous consciousness and those on the other side. Knowledge of those on the other side is the domain of pure or "transcendental" philosophy, distinguished from simple reflection, representation, and undisciplined flights of fancy.

This is one source of Maurice's insistence on digging as the proper function of the theologian (or philosopher). Though it is entirely possible to live a reflective life on the level of spontaneous consciousness, the philosophical task is to dig beneath that level to the more fundamental ground of philosophical consciousness. Because Coleridge's imagery moves both ways, with transcendental philosophy appearing beyond the fringe of spontaneous thought and in the knowledge of its practitioners that "the potential works in them, even as the actual works on them,"[14] it has the effect of collapsing inward and outward, subjective and objective. The organs of sense are framed for a corresponding world of sense. We all share these organs and the world with which they correspond. The organs of spirit are framed for a corresponding world of spirit. Though the organs exist in all people, they are not equally developed in all. Their appearance, Coleridge says, is disclosed in the moral being.

Associating the actual with organs of sense and the potential with organs of spirit lays the groundwork for a theory of moral development as well as a theory of moral education. While the moral being is disclosed as it crosses the boundary between the two worlds, most of our living is done in the world of sense.

This is probably not Kant, but Platonism of a distinctly Cambridge variety. The philosopher's task is to dig through the surface to the solid ground beneath. The ethical-political task is to bring the sensory world in which we do most of our living into the closest possible correspondence with another world toward which our spiritual development is directed. We live in this world turned toward another.

By now, this cave is so full of echoes that tracing the source of a sound is exceedingly difficult. Reference to the curve of a life sounds like Luther's distinction between life curved toward God and life curved toward self. But Augustinian sources permeate backgrounds common to Kant and Maurice as well as Luther, and behind all of them is a Platonic image of education as turning the soul.

Coleridge locates the certainty of our knowledge in affirmation of the immediate that dwells in every person. Though it dwells in every person, consciousness of it does not. Language, the medium of "ordinary" communication, plays off the surfaces that constitute matter, like smoke and mirrors or shadows on the inside surface of a cave.

Recall that matter has no inward. The medium of the depth, however, is freedom. To understand both Coleridge and Maurice, we must think carefully about the significance of freedom as a medium of communication. Both thinkers bring it to bear on sectarianism. Coleridge says that "we have imprisoned our own conceptions by the lines, which we have drawn, in order to exclude the conceptions of others."[15] We live, therefore, not in a cave but in a labyrinth of closets of our own making. Coleridge's advice, which he did not always follow, is a more practical version of Hegel's negation of the negation. "I find," he says, "that most sects are reasonable in a good part of what they advance, but not in what they deny."[16] When we turn to Maurice in the next chapter, we will see that he took this advice to heart in his most important writing. Coleridge's advice may provide a basis on which to elaborate grammars, logics, and rhetorics of freedom, necessary if freedom is to be a medium of communication in the "spiritual" world analogous to language as a medium of communication in the "material" one.

To the extent that we live in a "material" world oriented toward a "spiritual" one, we live in necessity toward freedom. That is a key to understanding Coleridge's critical theory, in which active imagination forms poetry out of the material, language, in which it works, toward the medium, freedom, in which it lives.

Before turning to Coleridge's critical theory, however, a few more words about the second burst of philosophical speculation.

Early in this chapter, I hinted that Coleridge would collapse epistemological and ontological questions. He does this clearly in his articulation of transcendental philosophy, folding ethical questions into the mix as well. The postulate of philosophy, the ground from which it begins, he says, is "the heaven-descended know thyself."[17] This injunction is simultaneously practical and speculative: philosophy is not only a science of reason or understanding (epistemology), and not only a science of morals (ethics), but also a science of being (ontology). Its primary ground cannot be either merely speculative or merely practical; it must be both at the same time.

Knowledge rests on "the coincidence of an object with a subject." The objective Coleridge calls Nature, the subjective he calls intelligence. Intelligence is representative, Nature represented. Knowledge is an act that consists in "a reciprocal concurrence of both," in which the two are so instantly united that we cannot determine which takes priority.[18] Two possibilities exist: either the objective is taken as first and we have to account for the coincidence of the subjective; or the subjective is taken as first and we have to account for the coincidence of the objective. Coleridge takes these as two equally important poles of fundamental science. In both cases, we are confronted with a union of opposites in which Nature is infused with intelligence, while intelligence is infused with Nature. Coleridge maintains that this is neither idealism nor materialism, but realism. He promises to demonstrate this at length in the same undelivered future work mentioned earlier in the chapter.

Though he does not deliver the finished work, Coleridge gives us ten theses from which the imagination is derived as a basis for critical theory. In these theses, he maintains that to know is in its essence an active verb; that truth is either derivative or immediate; that the only immediate truth is an absolute identity of subject and object, of finite and infinite. That immediate truth or absolute identity, which Coleridge refers to as spirit, self, or self-consciousness, is not a kind of being but a kind of knowing.

On the basis of this immediate truth that is a kind of knowing, Coleridge distinguishes imagination from fancy. He further distinguishes imagination as primary or secondary. Primary imagination is "the living Power and prime Agent of all human Perception,"[19] a repetition of the eternal act of creation. Secondary imagination is an echo, differing from primary imagination only in degree; it dissolves in order to recreate. Both varieties of imagination differ from objects in that they are active, while objects are fixed. Objects live to the extent that they are infused with vital imagination. Fancy is a mode of memory that "must receive all its materials ready made from the law of association."[20] Fancy lives in the spontaneous consciousness of the sensory world. It reflects passively, like a mirror, and it does not create. Imagination lives in the philosophical consciousness of the spiritual world. It reflects actively, recapitulating the creative act by breathing life into dead matter. Primary imagination is the soul of the world.

4. Essential Poetry

Early in *Biographia Literaria*, Coleridge defines essential poetry as that which we not only read with pleasure but return to with pleasure, and that which cannot be translated into other words of the same language without loss of significance. The image of return highlights the extent to which poetic genius consists in a continuously present undercurrent rather than a separate and transitory excitement. Keeping in mind the image of active imagination as the soul of the world, we see that this is another way of pointing to the sustaining power of poetry as well as establishing the sustained attention of criticism. Critical judgment rests not in reaction to accidental failures or shortcomings, but in careful exploration of qualities essential to the whole body of a poet's work.

That Coleridge grounds poetry and criticism in sustained attention to the essential qualities of a whole body of work is indicative of the close connection he saw between poetry and philosophy, and between these two and imagination. Poetic genius carries the feelings of childhood into the powers of adulthood, combining the child's sense of wonder with a lifetime of experience. Poetry and philosophy rescue universally accepted truths from impotence by continually making them new, digging beneath the surface to depths that are inexhaustible. This understanding grows out of conversation with William Wordsworth regarding two cardinal points of poetry, reported at the beginning of Chapter 14: "the power of exciting the sympathy of the reader by a faithful adherence to the truth of nature, and the power of giving the interest of novelty by the modifying colors of imagination."[21] These cardinal points are related to the distinction Coleridge draws between fancy and imagination. A simple mirroring of the sensuous world (fancy) would quickly degenerate into banality, reproducing the world without transforming it. But, because imagination is active, it makes the world new.

Philosophical discussion proceeds by distinction, not division. The philosophical and poetic process of distinction employs the two-step combinatorial activity of imagination discussed earlier, combining active and passive dimensions in a serpentine movement. Truth is distinguished into its component parts, and the unity of these parts is conceptually restored. Just as a leap requires that one defy gravity and submit to it, the process of philosophy requires distinction and unity if it is first to get off the ground and then return to it.

The proper distinction between poetry and prose is relevant to the relationship between poetry and philosophy. A poem is composed of the same elements as a prose composition, but a difference exists in form as well as object. "Object" does not refer so much to what a piece of writing is about as to the end toward which it is directed. Prose is characterized by having truth as its immediate end, with pleasure as a possible secondary result. It is primarily concerned with knowing, understood in terms of communication as transmission of information. It is only secondarily concerned with feeling. But poetry is marked by its primary concern with pleasure. A poem is

> that species of composition, which is opposed to works of science, by proposing for its immediate object pleasure, not truth; and from all other species (having *this* object in common with it) it is discriminated by proposing to itself such delight from the *whole*, as is compatible with a distinct gratification from each component *part*.[22]

That pleasure is poetry's primary object does not diminish truth's importance. Nothing can permanently please if it does not "contain in itself the reason why it is so, and not otherwise."[23] Attention must be sustained, not sporadic. If the form of a composition is detachable from its object, it is nothing more than a vehicle by which to get at the object. One vehicle may serve this purpose as well as another, though none will serve it perfectly. If composition and object are inextricably connected, then neither object nor composition is expendable or exchangeable. Prose gestures toward truth, and it may carry us along some way toward it. If so, it will impart pleasure. Poetry embodies truth in its form as well as its end. To the extent that poetry succeeds, pleasure is its end and its embodiment is truth.

The distinction between poetry and prose is not a distinction between poetry and philosophy. Because poetry is uniquely concerned with wholeness, it is the proper language of philosophy. Philosophical prose will necessarily be fragmentary and depend on poetry for its composition and its comprehension.

A legitimate poem is one "the parts of which mutually support and explain each other; all in their proportion harmonizing with, and supporting the purpose and known influences of metrical arrangement."[24] Harmony is a critical standard by which to judge the legitimacy of a composition. If it does not sing, it is not a poem.

Which leads to the question of the poet. The poet "brings the whole soul…into activity,"[25] harmonizing discordant qualities by the power of imagination. The poet, in short, is an embodied poem.

In the discussion of "common" language that Coleridge and Wordsworth initiated with *Lyrical Ballads,* poetics and politics interpenetrate. An ideal polity, like an ideal poet, embodies poetry. Every part supports and explains every other; every part and every relation harmonizes with and supports the whole. Wordsworth's confidence in the "common" language is a potentially democratic application of this social theory modified by Coleridge. The modification is a critique that illuminates limits that Coleridge and Maurice place on democratic politics.

Wordsworth maintained in his preface to *Lyrical Ballads* that language taken from real life is the proper diction for poetry and that this language constitutes natural human conversation. Coleridge offers three objections. First, the observation is applicable only in a limited class of poetry: it is true of some poems, but not all. Second, its application in this limited class is commonplace, not a subject for argument. Third, it is at best useless and at worst harmful when applied as a rule.

Coleridge does not object to the claim that the language of poetry is the language of real life. He is quite consistent in his insistence that poetic language is the most real language, closest to the freedom he identifies as the medium of the spiritual world toward which our lives in the sensual world are turned. But the claim is sometimes interpreted to mean that poetry should be written in "rustic" or "vulgar" language. Where Wordsworth represents conversational speech, he recasts it in poetic form and so refines it. This, Coleridge argues, is precisely what poetry should do: seek not the commonest language but the greatest refinement of the common speech. The poet's task (admirably executed by Wordsworth even where his theory contradicts his practice) is the turning of soul in refinement of language, one instance of the digging discussed earlier with regard to philosophic consciousness. This is why the observation is a commonplace in the class of poetry where it applies: Wordsworth's experiments with common subjects and common speech are undeniably real language, but they are not transcriptions of common speech. Such transcription is one disastrous result of a mechanical application of Wordsworth's observation as a rule. Creativity is sacrificed, the poetry does not sing, and souls turn toward the sensuous rather than the spiritual world.

5. A Contribution to the Formation of an Age

Like *Biographia Literaria, Aids to Reflection* is an important part of the record of Coleridge's passage through the struggles of his age, not so much a case against the age as a participant's contribution to its formation. Though its publication was met with critical silence, its influence on succeeding generations of theological and political theorists gives it an undeniable historic significance.

In keeping with Maurice's reading, the particular questions with which Coleridge struggled are less important than the shape of the struggle itself, though in some cases the two are inseparable.

Coleridge outlines his purpose in the Preface, where he describes four objects, in order of importance:

1. "To direct the reader's attention to the value of the science of words, their use and abuse, and the incalculable advantages attached to the habit of using them appropriately, and with a distinct knowledge of their primary, derivative, and metaphorical senses."[26] Coleridge speaks of living words and extends Horne Tooke's image of words as the wheels of thought with reference to Ezekiel. Wheels of the intellect Coleridge acknowledges them to be, but also wheels that go where the spirit goes. Here as in *Biographia Literaria*, Coleridge looks to the power of words as a key to keeping head and heart, soul and body, together.

2. "To establish the *distinct* characters of Prudence, Morality, and Religion: and to impress the conviction, that though the second requires the first, and the third contains and supposes both the former; yet still Moral Goodness is other and more than Prudence, or the Principle of Expediency; and Religion more and higher than Morality."[27] Here Coleridge joins a debate of particular importance against the background described in Chapter One: contrary to the flattening tendency of Political Economy as it gained a toehold in every branch of nineteenth-century British thought, religion could not be reduced to morality, and neither could be reduced to prudence equated with expediency. Properly distinguishing these words means outlining an alternative to Political Economy, the alternative John Stuart Mill noted in his encounters with Maurice at the London Debating Society.

3. "To substantiate and set forth at large the momentous distinction between REASON and understanding...to establish the position, that whoever transfers to the understanding the primacy due to the Reason, loses the one and spoils the other."[28] *Aids to Reflection* may be read as an attack on the rationalism of early nineteenth-century British thought, but only if we insist that the attack is directed not at reason but at the distortion of its meaning that results from failure to properly distinguish it from understanding. In Coleridge's view, rationalism abandons reason in favor of sensation. This undermines reflection and responsibility as well as freedom.

4. "To exhibit a full and consistent Scheme of the Christian Dispensation, and more largely of all the *peculiar* doctrines of the Christian Faith."[29] *Aids to Reflection* may be read as Coleridge's apology for Anglican

orthodoxy, but only if we insist that the "apology" is an exposition of the relationship between mystery and reason that is another version of the attack on mechanistic philosophy, and hardly the orthodoxy of mainline nineteenth-century Anglicanism.

The difficulty of the text, and one of its legacies to Maurice, resides in Coleridge's insistence on pursuing all four objects at once. Proper distinctions are displayed in practice, in a labyrinth of notes, references, and asides that (as Coleridge coyly observes in a postscript at the end of a note) don't require an apology to readers who have been paying attention, "it being understood beforehand that the sauce and the garnish are to occupy the greater part of the dish."[30] That is an "apology" placed where those who expect an apology are least likely to find it. Impatient readers will have abandoned the notes (if not the text) well before this point, and where those who know an apology is not required are most likely to encounter it as a good joke, another spice added to bring out the flavor of the sauce. The entree carrying all this sauce and garnish is Cambridge Platonism, in aphorisms taken from Archbishop Robert Leighton, Henry More, and others.

Coleridge's method is outlined most clearly and most appropriately in a long note in the middle of an even longer comment on an aphorism. The subject of the aphorism, taken from Leighton, is redemption—specifically the distance beyond nature's reach of a crucified Savior. Here is a reality that extends far beyond the reach of understanding, but it is not, Coleridge insists, irrational. The distinction is critical for Coleridge, explicit in the third, implicit in the first and second objects of the *Aids*. Where the distinction is not properly drawn, we cannot hope to penetrate beyond surface phenomena. Drawing it is a matter of method, more explicitly outlined here than in *Biographia Literaria*.

The method, which bears a family resemblance to Kant (and therefore Hegel and Marx), though it is not derivative, is built on a triadic structure derived from a Pythagorean understanding of the geometry of the line. A line may be drawn from a point midway between two extremes, "indifferent" with regard to the extremes, identifiable with either, identical to neither. Applied to logic, the extremes may be called *thesis* and *antithesis*. The midpoint, equally identifiable with either pole, Coleridge calls *mesothesis*. This mesothesis may be conceived as both thesis and antithesis, but not at the same time. Relative to the thesis, the mesothesis is equal to the antithesis; relative to the antithesis, the mesothesis is equal to the thesis. The mesothesis does not bring thesis and antithesis together, but occupies and defines middle ground while it is pulled from moment to moment one way or the other. The third term in popular expositions of Kant and Hegel is *synthesis*, which, by bringing together thesis and antithesis, comprehends both. Coleridge maintains, however, that this convergence depends on a comprehensive *prothesis* present before thesis, antithesis, and mesothesis.

He imagines the Pythagoreans rendering the constructions of pure mathematics applicable to philosophy by generating the line from a point which it does not contain, independent of the line, transcendent to its production. The assumption of this transcendent generative point is the prothesis. With its assumption in relation to the line, four relations of thought are expressed: prothesis, or identity of thesis and antithesis; thesis, or position; antithesis, or opposition; and mesothesis, or indifference. Synthesis adds composition. Prothesis, thesis, antithesis, mesothesis, and synthesis together make up a "noetic pentad" which describes the rhythm of distinction and comprehension characteristic of reason. Below or behind distinction lies the unity of prothesis; above or beyond it lies the unity of synthesis. More explicitly than Kant, Coleridge connects analytic and synthetic, practical and "pure," reason in what he calls "the five most general forms or preconceptions of constructive logic."[31]

With this, Coleridge returns to the *Idea*, which is neither an impression on the senses nor a mere abstraction from sensory data. Beginning with the absolutely real as prothesis, the subjectively real as thesis, and the objectively real as antithesis, he identifies *Idea* as mesothesis. Conceived as in the subject, *Idea* is an object; conceived as in the object, it is a subject. This is the two-step serpentine movement of active imagination that I described earlier in discussion of *Biographia Literaria*.

The distinction between understanding and reason, arguably the most important contribution of *Aids to Reflection*, is certainly its most important contribution to F.D. Maurice's method.

Coleridge describes the difference between reason and understanding as a difference in kind, and he outlines it most explicitly in the section of *Aids to Reflection* devoted to "spiritual religion indeed." The outline follows a comment on an aphorism from Leighton:

> Faith elevates the soul not only above sense and sensible things, but above reason itself. As reason corrects the errors which sense might occasion, so supernatural faith corrects the errors of natural reason judging according to sense.[32]

Coleridge laments a pervasive tendency in British thought, evident in the aphorism from Leighton, to include two faculties under the one heading of "reason," which, under the influence of Locke, is always derivative from sensation and opposite to faith. In order to properly distinguish these faculties, Coleridge proposes a consistent application of two terms, reason and understanding. Understanding is discursive, derivative, and reflective. Reason is fixed, substantial, and contemplative. Understanding is "the faculty by which we reflect and generalize." Coleridge describes understanding as a three-step process relative to but only partly dependent on sensation: attention, abstraction, and generalization. The first step is passive: our attention is appropriated. The second is active: we attend selectively. The third is comparative and synthetic. As a whole, the function or end of the understanding is generalization of sensory data in the construction of names. The understanding is "a faculty judging according to sense," but it is also an active faculty that constructs categories. Reason, on the other hand, is "the source of necessary and universal principles, according to which the notices of the senses are either affirmed or denied" and "the power by which we are enabled to draw from particular and contingent appearances universal and necessary conclusions."[33] Understanding is dependent on and posterior to sensation, while reason is independent and anterior.

Coleridge objects to the essential passivity and determinism of Lockean "reason," not so much a term as a confusion that, because it conflates two faculties that differ in kind, is not even half right. The conflation of faculties results in a language of necessity that undermines freedom and communication.

Neither understanding nor reason is simply passive. Both proceed by the serpentine rhythm of action and passion described in *Biographia Literaria* with reference to imagination. Understanding abstracts on the basis of reason and sensation; resting on wholes, it weaves parts together. Reason is the whole by which understanding operates on sensation. The digger combines both but does not conflate them. This is partly a matter of the direction, partly a matter of the operation of thought. In Leighton's aphorism, reason corrects sensation, faith corrects reason, and our soul is lifted above both. From sensation through reason to transcendence, the soul is a butterfly that the world sends fluttering on its way. But Coleridge, a digger like Maurice, looks for ground. From transcendent reason through sensation and understanding toward comprehension and communication, the soul, grounded in the world, grounds the world in God.

Whether we are reading Coleridge or Maurice, direction is important. Neither is reactive, and we would be mistaken to understand either, finally, as making a case against his age. Coleridge said of himself that he went further than the Unitarians and came out on the other side. The same might be said of Maurice. Neither simply reacted to the world. Both burrowed into it with an intensity that grounded their criticisms and enabled them to pass through the struggles of the age rather than being caught up in them.

The path Maurice traces through Coleridge's writing is a chronological but selective reading that passes from poetry through journalism to metaphysics and political philosophy. This is instructive, because it so closely parallels Maurice's own career and because, in spite of appearances to the contrary, it is not a movement away from poetry or contemporary affairs. For Maurice, it is a potentially instructive record of a passage through the struggles of an age.

In this chapter, I have drawn the circle more tightly, focusing on *Biographia Literaria* and *Aids to Reflection*. That is not to diminish the importance of the other works Maurice cites, but to pay tribute to a consistency in Coleridge that is sometimes obscured by fascination with his relationship to electoral politics and to defer to more comprehensive studies of Coleridge's philosophy that are readily available.[34] That Coleridge is most useful where he is creative and imaginative, least useful where he is reactive, is a practical confirmation of his theory. We should not expect too much of what he writes in recoil at the excesses of revolutionary movements, and we should not allow such writing to divert attention from the constant themes embodied most fully in those two major works. Coleridge's *The Statesman's Manual* and *On the Constitution of Church and State*, which Maurice includes in his record of Coleridge's passage, should not be read primarily as evidence of a political turn. The first is ostensibly a sermon to the ruling class on how to read the Bible and apply it as a guide in the practice of politics. Maurice described it as less developed than the other works cited, but learned a great deal from it about reading history philosophically and was prompted by it to attend to the task of broadening the audience for informed and responsible political discourse. He also found in *The Statesman's Manual* an approach to reading the Bible consistent with the approach to reading a poem developed at length in *Biographia Literaria*. Both are to be encountered as organic wholes, not collections of fragments, which recalls Benjamin Jowett's observation that we should read the Bible the way we read any other book. The second is not an apology for the established church so much as the record of a struggle with the perennial problem of clearing a space for the practice of freedom on a field where particular powers compete to become absolute. As I noted in Chapter One, that is a familiar theme for theological and philosophical discussion in Britain, and Maurice appropriates it in his relationship with the established church. This puts Maurice and Coleridge at odds with a political tradition embodied most fully in Thomas Paine. But, as I noted in Chapter One, the quarrel centers on mechanism more than monarchy. Though Coleridge and Maurice are monarchists, they can agree with the anti-monarchist Paine on the need to use political structures to limit the actualization of potentially absolute powers.

For Maurice, as for Coleridge, electoral politics is a distraction from serious political engagement. They watched with alarm as a mechanistic-utilitarian philosophy permeated the whole spectrum of British political thought. They saw that philosophical orientation as the enemy of freedom, and they were alarmed by its ability to feed on popular political discourse. As writers, they found their most likely places in electoral politics defined journalistically. They occupied those places for a time but grew impatient and generally contemptuous of the possibilities such places afforded. The mechanistic-utilitarian philosophy thrived on the human fragmentation accelerated by popular journalism's anonymity and superficiality. Serious political engagement demanded attention to the roots, the constitution, of society. Hence, the metaphysical turn, and, in Maurice, the maturation of socialism from cooperation to education.

Three

A SYSTEM THAT IS ALL DOOR

The Kingdom of Christ, Maurice's first major theological work and the work for which he is most often remembered, was originally published as *Letters to a Member of the Society of Friends*, addressed to Rev. Samuel Clark and issued in twelve parts beginning in January 1837. It was reissued in a three-volume edition in 1838 as *The Kingdom of Christ: or Hints on the Principles, Ordinances, and Constitution of the Catholic Church in Letters to a Member of the Society of Friends*, then revised and reissued in a second edition as *The Kingdom of Christ; or, Hints to a Quaker respecting the Principles, Constitution, and Ordinances of the Catholic Church* in 1842. The second edition included a dedication to Samuel Taylor Coleridge's son, Rev. Derwent Coleridge, in which Maurice traced his intellectual debt to Coleridge in some detail. As Maurice later wrote, the text was addressed to Quakers but written for Anglicans, partly as a reaction to the high Church Oxford Movement (specifically, Pusey's tract on baptism), which had taken Maurice's earlier "Subscription No Bondage" as evidence that he was a member of their party. At the time Maurice wrote his second letter to Clark, dealing with baptism and responding to Pusey, the Oxford party had nominated him for a professorship in Political Economy as part of a plan to fill all the major positions at the University with members of their party. They were so infuriated with what Maurice wrote on baptism that they rescinded their votes in support of his candidacy, which was then withdrawn.[1]

1. A Universal Church

Near the end of the dedication, Maurice describes a throughly Coleridgean vision of a universal Church "not built upon human inventions or human faith, but upon the very nature of God" and the union God has formed with humankind, a Church revealed to humankind "as a fixed and eternal reality by means which infinite wisdom had itself devised."[2] In contrast to the prevailing emphasis on humanity's fallen nature, Maurice assumes that humanity's unity with God is a more fundamental reality than the alienation resulting from the Fall. Alienation is a radical distortion. The more "natural" condition of humanity is unity with, not alienation from, God. The Gospel proclaims that God's unity with humanity is not only coming, but is always present. Human beings "are not to gain a kingdom hereafter, but are put in possession of it now, and through their chastisements and the oppositions of their evil nature they are to learn its character and enter into its privileges...." Love has been made manifest to humankind, which has "been brought into fellowship with it...."[3]

Like his Unitarian contemporary James Martineau, Maurice articulates an understanding of the Incarnation as true of humankind inclusively, not Jesus exclusively. He does not stop at belief in an historical event, but pushes the concept of the event beyond its limit, toward its origin, where it is a powerful symbol of the reality of a catholic church and a humanity in which God is fully present. In Coleridge's sense, the Church is an *idea*, antecedent to human experience and sensation, not consequent. It has much in common with Coleridge's understanding, articulated in *The Constitution of Church and State*, of the Christian Church as distinct from Christianity and National Church. For Maurice, as for Coleridge, the universal Church stands opposite the world understood as an aggregate of particulars. That opposition is understood precisely in terms of aggregation directs Maurice's attention through particulars. The universal is not an aggregate of particulars, but a ground under particulars. Not a particular itself, the universal is wholly present in every particular.

Having learned from Coleridge to read history philosophically, Maurice surveys religious and philosophical positions developed since the Reformation, highlighting their positive principles and the contradictions that exist between those principles and the systems that have been devised to embody them. Though the systems are diverse, all obscure or distort the principles with which they are associated. The survey is intended to demonstrate that this is the case and to suggest why.

True to his audience, Maurice begins with the Quaker principle of an inward light, which he sees as an expression of God's unity with humanity. Human beings are twofold, having "inclinations towards sensible things" while at the same time "being united to the divine Word" by trusting in whom we "may rise above these inclinations and attain to a spiritual life and communion."[4] By asserting the universality of the inward light, this principle proclaims the reality of God's union with every person.

From this Quaker principle, Maurice proceeds to Protestant emphases on justification (Luther), election (Calvin), and Scripture (Zwingli), each of which is a positive aspect of the spiritual society. Assertion of an "Absolute Will" is characteristic of the Reformers, while assertion of a relation between the Divine Word and creatures is characteristic of the Quakers.[5] God is simultaneously Absolute and Immanent.

These principles are extended in the Unitarian emphasis on unity. Maurice maintains that, while Quakerism and pure Protestantism belong to "the region of individual life and experience," Unitarianism leads us "from self-reflection to thoughts about nature and God." God's relationship to humanity is at once individual and communal.

The principles "asserted by the religious societies which have been formed in Europe since the Reformation are solid and imperishable," but "the systems in which these principles have been embodied were faulty in their origin, have been found less and less to fulfill their purpose as they have grown older, and are now exhibiting the most manifest indications of approaching dissolution."[6] The Quaker principle of the universality of the inward light is contradicted by a sectarian Quaker system. The Lutheran system "does not bear witness for the all-importance of that fact which Luther asserted to be all-important; ...it teaches us to believe in justification by faith instead of to believe in a Justifier; ...it substitutes for Christ a certain notion or scheme of Christianity."[7] The idea of election is dogmatized in the Calvinist system in a way that drains the individual will and shifts attention from the Incarnation. Insofar as Zwinglianism has influenced the Protestant system as a whole, reverence for the Bible has been transformed into a Biblicism that replaces Christianity. Likewise, the Unitarian principle of unity and universality is contradicted in the limited, sectarian polity of the Unitarian system. In each case, "system" shifts the focus from the fact of the Incarnation to dogmas about the nature of God and humanity.

Maurice summarizes his exploration by asserting "that the principles of Fox, of Luther, of the Unitarians are too strong, too vital, to bear the imprisonment to which they have been subjected in the different systems which have been invented for them...."[8] The emphasis here is on invention and containment. Systems are artificial aggregates intended to contain principles. When they are taken not as artificially constructed aggregates of fragments but as naturally given wholes, the result is, inevitably, distortion, and principles are not "contained" but imprisoned.

Maurice distinguishes himself from what he describes as a growing philosophical conviction that "systems, religions, churches, are dying out, but that they have been the clothing of certain important ideas which will survive their extinction, and which it is the business of wise men to note, preserve, and perhaps furnish with a new vesture...."[9] He says that "if this book means anything," he must be "directly opposed" to such a system. Maurice is not interested in finding a least common denominator (or a greatest possible aggregate) to be preserved apart from Personality. "Principles," he says, do not become more vital when "they have lost their religious and personal character, and have been translated into the terms of a philosophical theory." Instead, at that point, they "attain the perfection of the impotence and insignificance to which hitherto they have been but partially reduced."[10] The spiritual society is not to be apprehended in movement away from religious and personal character, but in affirmation of that character: "every modern attempt to construct a universal society has been defeated" by the assertion of human wills. The true universal society must be one which neither overlooks the existence of those wills, nor considers them as an inconvenient and accidental interruption to its workings, as a friction to be regretted and allowed for, but which assumes them as the very principle and explanation of its existence.[11]

It is equally impossible for human beings "to be content with a spiritual society which is not universal, and with a universal society which is not spiritual." For Maurice, the spiritual and universal society "must be that constitution, by virtue of which we realize that there is a humanity, that we form a kind."[12] The universal society is more real than anything else. The problem is not how to "create" it but how to live in such a way as to affirm its reality.

Maurice's view of this society depends on an understanding of "spiritual constitution" derived from a reading of Scripture that owes much to Coleridge's first "lay sermon." Maurice begins by distinguishing system from method. System indicates "that which is most opposed to life, freedom, variety." Method indicates "that without which they cannot exist." This distinction allows him to concur with the critical judgment that the Bible is unsystematic. There is no system in the Bible, but there is a "method." Its truth resides "not in the words but in the history."[13] For Maurice, as for Coleridge, the Bible is the history of God's being-in-the-world with God's people. The Scriptural view of spiritual constitution emerges from that history.

Covenant, which Maurice takes to be the central theme of Hebrew Scripture, transcends individuals and individual choice. That God is related to humankind and made known through human relations was Abraham's faith, and on that basis Maurice credits Abraham with being "the beginner of the Church on earth." This suggests that a Church founded on God's relationship with humankind is not necessarily a Christian church and that a Church founded on relationship could not be clearly exhibited in one individual faithful person. As Coleridge suggested, while Christianity is invisible, the Church is public.

In Abraham's case, Maurice maintains, the Church was exhibited through a family. Although all members of the family of Abraham were included in the covenant, Maurice says, not all were faithful. He points to the faithful Joseph and his unfaithful brothers. It would have been a simple matter for Joseph to separate himself from the unfaithful, but that, Maurice points out, is not what the history relates. If Joseph had separated himself, he "would have founded a society which was built upon choice, not upon relationship."[14] But the Church Maurice reads in Hebrew Scripture grows out of relationship, not choice.

Maurice's reading does not stop at family. He says "part of the promise" was that the Jews would move beyond the patriarchal state. He sees this movement embodied in the nation. This is revealed in several ways: the commandments declare the existence of a "Being from whom all law came"; the tabernacle affirms the presence of this Being; the family witnesses to relationship between

God and worshipers; the priesthood witnesses that this relationship might be realized in a representative; the national constitution contributes to an awareness of evil arising from violations of relationship with God and other persons; and the sacrifices testify to the restoration of relationship contingent upon giving up of self-will. In short, the nation exists as a broad manifestation of relationship which testifies to humanity's relationship with God. Maurice summarizes his position by saying that "human relationships are not artificial types of something divine, but are actually the means and the only means, through which" human beings ascend "to any knowledge of the divine; and...every breach of a human relation, as it implies a violation of the higher law, so also is a hindrance and barrier to the perception of that higher law,—the drawing a veil" between the spirit of humanity and humanity's God.[15] Persons attain knowledge of God in human relationships. The Scriptural record indicates that those relationships are familial and national, though they are not merely familial or national.

Maurice sees the union between Godhead and humanity as the central message of Christian Scripture. This is conveyed in the record of acts, especially the act of Incarnation. This act, coming in the history of covenant, most clearly reveals the unity of God with humanity. This is Maurice's point when he says that the ultimate basis of a universal society is a Name. That name is the symbol of union; it is the reality of union that joins persons to persons and joins humanity to God.

In summarizing his perception of the Scriptural view of the spiritual constitution, Maurice distinguishes two parts: the spiritual society is united by family relationships and by locality. This is a restatement of the realization that the Church is familial and national. Maurice builds on this restatement by pointing to the dependence of both parts on a third, which may have one of two forms. One form, which Maurice labels "the world," is destructive of the family and national principles; the other, "the Church," nurtures them. That is the key mark of distinction of the Church. While the world is an aggregate founded on human will, the Church, like the family and the nation, is founded on relationship.

Maurice's three parts encompass human relationships at all levels, with the crucial level being relationship to God. Human relationships are the "type" of humanity's relationship to God, and whether they are "whole" depends on the realization of that relationship. Its denial by "the world" in the assertion of human will results in, and is reflected in, broken communal relationships. Its affirmation by "the Church" in the realization of human relatedness to God results in, and is reflected in, healthy communal relationships.

Maurice's reading of the spiritual constitution, like Coleridge's reading, imparts a sacramental character to family and nation that demands even greater caution at the beginning of the twenty-first century than it did in the middle of the nineteenth. The danger of their readings lies not so much in the sacramental character of human relationships, though no reader at the beginning of the twenty-first century is likely to deny that the power of those relationships carries an associated danger, as in the pervasive confusion of particular with universal.

Cautions against that confusion (as Coleridge and Maurice note) are clearly articulated in the Hebrew prophetic tradition, especially as it relates to priestly tradition. Coleridge develops this in his proposal for a national clerisy, and Maurice incorporates that proposal and the cautions of the prophetic tradition in his educational theory, to which I will devote detailed discussion in Chapter Four. This potential for confusion was a central factor in shaping the understanding Coleridge and Maurice shared of the political significance of education and the limits of democracy.

Maurice's philosophical reading of history turns into a sacramental reading of the spiritual constitution that leads to a close examination of the two rites, baptism and Eucharist, identified by Protestants and Catholics as sacraments.

Not surprisingly, he looks through the more than eighteen hundred year history of baptism as a rite among "different tribes of the most different origin and character" to its meaning as a universal rite of the Church. The fact, he says, does not need to be established, but the meaning requires special attention. For Maurice, this meaning is not so much a matter of connection between the particularities of the tribes that have practiced the rite as between each particular practice of the rite and the revelation of a Kingdom founded on the union of God with humanity:

> Even though baptism were enjoined as a rite by our Lord Himself, yet if it were appointed in such terms as leave us at liberty to suppose that it was merely accidental to the general purpose of his advent, we cannot prove an identity between the universal society which acknowledges it now and the one which he founded.[16]

Maurice's interpretation is informed by his vision of the universal Church. He seeks to reveal a connection between the universal society established in the union of God with humanity and the rite of baptism. Baptism, for Maurice, is a celebration of an already existing unity, not a means of entrance into that unity.

In establishing the connection, Maurice goes directly to the Gospel accounts. Beginning with John the Baptist, he points out that "baptism is connected with a spiritual act, that of repentance; with a spiritual promise, that of remission; with the announcement of a kingdom; with an intimation that the kingdom should not merely be composed of the children of Abraham." At the least, he says, the Scriptural record of John's activity establishes that baptism "was the preparation for the Gospel." This alone does not establish it as more than a preparation, so Maurice goes on to examine the Scriptural account of Jesus's own baptism:

Jesus Himself descends into the water, and as He comes out of it, a voice from heaven proclaims Him the well beloved Son, and the Spirit descends upon Him in bodily shape. The announcement then that the Divine man, the king of men, had really appeared, was, according to the Gospels, connected with Baptism. And this same Baptism they speak of as the beginning of our Lord's public ministry....[17]

Baptism is more than a preparation, and it has a connection with the establishment of the Kingdom. But, Maurice admits, "this might have been necessary to mark the leader; it need not have any application to his disciples."[18] This possibility is explored and discounted by reference to Jesus' teaching. He appointed Apostles to baptize. He told Nicodemus that a person must be born of water and of the spirit to enter the kingdom of heaven. This is further reinforced by the post-resurrection injunction to his disciples to go and baptize. Maurice believes that the Scriptural evidence points to baptism as a sign of the universal kingdom; the eighteen hundred years of practice become infinitely important.

That Maurice sees baptism as a celebration of a present reality is further evidenced in his description of the young Christian convert's "battle":

Your foes are not hindering you from obtaining a blessing; they are hindering you from entering into the fruition of one that has been obtained for you; they will laugh at you for pretending that it is yours; they will tell you that you must not claim it. But in the strength of this covenant you must claim it; otherwise your life will be a lie.[19]

Because baptism is the sign of a blessing already obtained, and because "the kingdom of Christ was declared to be an everlasting kingdom," we who have received the sign are "in the same position," have "the same privileges," and are "under the same responsibilities, as those who lived eighteen hundred years ago."[20] This bears striking resemblance to Kierkegaard's claim that there is no disciple at second hand. And, in spite of the obvious differences between the two thinkers (especially with regard to the eighteen hundred years of practice), that seems to capture the essence of Maurice's idea of presence. Baptism is the sign of a present unity, a spiritual/universal society that is here and now. Where else would it be?

In considering the Eucharist, Maurice again points to the eighteen hundred plus years of practice of the rite. As with baptism, it is and has been practiced in the most diverse nations and tribes. And, although at the time of the Reformation the Eucharist was shifted away from its central position, the Reformers were still "compelled to make their views respecting this feast the characteristic and distinguishing feature of their systems." Universality of practice is supplemented in Maurice's argument by the central importance of this rite:

> in the nineteenth century there are not a few persons who, meditating on these different experiments, have arrived at this deep and inward conviction, that the question whether Christianity shall be a practical principle and truth..., or shall be exchanged for a set of intellectual notions or generalizations, depends mainly on the question whether the Eucharist shall or shall not be acknowledged and received as the bond of a universal life, and the means whereby [human beings] become partakers of it.[21]

As with baptism, the history of the practice of the rite does not need to be established, but its centrality and widespread practice call for careful examination of its meaning.

To describe the nature of Eucharist would be difficult, Maurice says, without entering into points of disagreement, but its origin is not a matter of dispute. Protestants, Catholics, and Orthodox all look to the words of institution as the ground on which it is established. But these words, according to Maurice, would be most easily explained as a hyperbolical call to remembrance, "unless there were some circumstances connected with the whole character of Him who spoke the words, with His other acts and purposes, with the time they were spoken, which determined them to a different sense."[22] Any explanation beyond simple remembrance must be grounded in the context of Jesus' ministry, not in the words themselves. This thought informs the remainder of Maurice's exploration.

The single most important contextual aspect Maurice considers is the person of Jesus of Nazareth, specifically the belief that he was the Son of God and the Son of Man. This links the Eucharist with the Incarnation and with the covenant history. If we accept the belief that Jesus was the Son of God and the Son of Man, we introduce a chain of implications which Maurice describes in detail.[23] We must consider Jesus' declaration that he is the way through which human beings "must come to the unseen Father," his description of his relationship to the disciples as a vine to its branches, his appointment of the disciples as the "messengers of these truths." We must remember Jesus' prayer that his disciples and all who "believe in him through their word might be one in Him as He and the Father were one," and we must recall the connection Jesus had established between these "mysterious words" and his death. This last connection brings to mind the whole covenant history and the Hebrew understanding of sacrifice. The connection is strengthened by the fact that the words of institution were spoken at "the most purely national and strictly sacrificial of all the feasts, that one which celebrated the first deliverance and establishment of the nation, and which recalled the fact that it was a nation based upon sacrifices in which every Jew realized the blessings" of the covenant.[24] Maurice asks "whether anyone who believed what we know the Apostles did believe respecting their Master, His Person, His kingdom, could attach any but the very highest significance to language concerning His body and blood."[25] The Eucharist is intrinsically connected with the person of Jesus understood as the revelation of God's presence with God's people. By that connection, it is joined to and informed by the covenant history of the Jewish people. The Eucharist is a celebration of God's presence, an embodiment of the conciliatory meaning of the Jewish sacrifice.

In discussing "origin" Maurice has trespassed on "nature." This carries with it the risk of being lost in disagreements of which he was aware and new disagreements that have proliferated since he wrote. But the key is Maurice's consistent belief that it is each practice as a sign of the idea beneath every practice, not an intellectual comprehension of all the particular practices, that matters. Incarnation, "the union of Godhead with human flesh,"[26] is the central reality; how one interprets that reality does not alter the fact of its existence. The Eucharist is a celebration of that fact, and, as such, it transcends differences, it proclaims union, and, like baptism, it affirms that we are in the same relationship with God as those who first celebrated the fact in this rite over eighteen hundred years ago.

Maurice's antipathy to system makes it difficult to elaborate an ecclesiological structure based on his thought. That is precisely what he would have wanted. His closing remarks from *The Kingdom of Christ* are illuminating:

> since a school, which should be formed to oppose all schools, must be of necessity more mischievous than any of them; and since a school, which pretended to amalgamate the doctrines of all other schools, would be, as I think, more mischievous than that, I do pray earnestly, that if any such schools should arise, they may come to nought; and that, if what I have written in this book should tend even in the least degree to favour the establishment of them, it may come to nought. On the other hand, if there be anything here which may help to raise [people] above their own narrow conceptions and mine, may lead them to believe that there is a way to that truth which is living and universal, and above us all, and that He who is Truth will guide them in that way, this which is from Him and not from me, I pray that He will bless. 'Let all thine enemies perish, O Lord'; all systems, schools, parties which have hindered [people] from seeing the largeness, and freedom, and glory of thy kingdom; 'but let them that love thee,' in whatever earthly mists they may at present be involved, 'be as the sun when he goeth forth in strength.[27]

Maurice offers no "system" to save the world, only the affirmation that it is saved. His vision exposes the arrogance of those who would establish unity by doctrinal agreement, by system, by rejection of those who disagree. To take upon oneself that kind of task is to assert, whether consciously or unconsciously, that the Kingdom has not come, that it is not among us or upon us. It is to deny God's presence with God's people and make the covenant history a lie.

2. The Spirit, the Body, the Communion of Saints

Maurice insisted on a universal Church, the reality of which illuminates doctrinal dispute, responsible human action, and worship. Doctrine, action, and worship are inextricably bound by the threefold reality affirmed in the third article of the Apostle's Creed: spirit, body, and communion. This is as important to Maurice's social theory and his pedagogy as to his theology. It is a key to understanding why social theory, pedagogy, and theology are one activity rather than three discrete bodies of knowledge. It may also be a key to understanding how Maurice simultaneously embraced Trinitarian orthodoxy, affirmed his Unitarian roots, and cultivated the deep respect for the Society of Friends evident in *The Kingdom of Christ*. He dealt with these issues in a series of sermons on the *Book of Common Prayer* that he preached in London in 1848, the very year in which Christian Socialism was born.

The dedication, preface, and introductory sermon concisely describe the structure and direction of the whole series.[28]

In the dedication, Maurice classes himself with those who "never have found or expect to find a home in any religious party, rest in any religious theory." Finding a home is a central concern for ethics; as Paul Lehmann pointed out in *Ethics in a Christian Context*, "ethics" is itself derived from *ethos*, which originally referred to a dwelling place for animals.[29] In this sense, as Lehmann implied, ethics is where we are at home. Maurice is convinced that Christians cannot find a home in "theory" or in "party;" but we are not thereby condemned to homelessness. We are directed to "making a home" as a critical ethical task and as a crucial concern for this series of sermons. In the process, we are directed to separate ourselves from separatist tendencies.

The preface begins with a statement of the occasion for the book: it is a response to the popular opinion that the Church of England is founded on a compromise. If that opinion is true, Maurice says, then he has "no right to offer [the prayers of the Church] to God or to ask honest people to join in offering them."[30] This is so because, in that case, our "home," the place from which we begin and in which we grow and are nurtured, would be built on something less than truth. Maurice suggests that it is time for everyone to declare whether this is how s/he understands the Church. The appearance of "compromise" serves as an occasion for decision. The question is cast not only in terms of the structure of the Prayer Book but also in terms of the perception of that structure.

Keeping the "compromise" in mind, Maurice explains that the sermons were delivered for laypersons to indicate why he could ask them to join with him in offering the prayers of the Church. They were published for young clergy and those preparing to become clergy to emphasize that they are potential restorers or destroyers of morality. Whether one is a "restorer" or a "destroyer" is largely dependent on how one answers the question regarding compromise. Those who see "compromise" are destroyers while those who do not are, potentially, restorers. "Restoration" is inclusive, while "destruction" is exclusive. Restoration demands action on principle; destruction involves conventionality, suspicion, fear, and partisanship.

In the introductory sermon, Maurice says that he wants to see what use we have been making of the yearly services of the Church. Speaking in terms of the "compromise," Maurice looks at the liturgy (which is allegedly "Papist") and the Articles (which are allegedly "Protestant"). He suggests that the two are seen as contradictory (or compromised) because their purposes are not adequately distinguished. In his view, they are generically distinct. The prayers, which are for all, focus on worship; the Articles, which are for a particular group of specialists, focus on theological study. Maurice calls for "the same distinction here which is recognized in every other department of thought between that which is common, real, living, and that which is special, dogmatical, technical."[31] On the basis of this distinction, he acknowledges a wide divergence in character between the liturgy and the Articles. If the distinction is not made, the two appear contradictory; if it is made, they appear complementary.

Of worship, Maurice says: "if we are wrong here, we are wrong altogether."[32] Maurice sees potential deliverance from exclusivity in worship, not in theological study. The two are mutually informative. The "special, dogmatical, technical" grows out of the "common, real, living." The "common, real, living" is the basis of unity. The "special, dogmatical, technical" is a useful tool when seen in context.

Worship may be characterized as action grounded in principle. For Maurice, the "noblest distinction" of our Prayers is that "they set out with assuming God to be a Father, and those that worship Him to be his children." The foundation is the "union of Godhead with human flesh." From that foundation, the liturgy and all effective moral action grow.

A distinction is drawn between reforming and corrupting action. Reforming action begins with the Incarnation. It emphasizes *Common* and does not become involved in "special pleading about the word '*us*'."[33] Corrupting action begins with the Fall. It is "conventional," "suspicious," "fearful," "partisan," "abstract," or "mystical," goes looking for heresy, and invariably finds it. Maurice's point, elaborated in the sermons that follow, is that "liturgical" action is "morally responsible" action.

Maurice's argument is anti-systematic but not unsystematic. It is more concerned with method than with system. He does not elaborate a set of general rules to be applied in specific cases, but describes a way of acting (a "style") which determines particular objective acts in particular objective cases.

Destructive ethics grows out of a perception of a foundation for the Church which is a compromise between contradictory positions. Grounded in contradiction, transforming "converse with God...into a lie," it transforms all things into a lie.[34] The foundation of destructive ethics is the Fall. The person who lives this ethics thinks of himself or herself as a creature essentially alienated from God. The alienation at the center determines all of existence. Actions are undertaken out of fear of punishment or expectation of reward.[35] They are calculated to appease a God perceived as essentially angry, inclined to punish unless persuaded to do otherwise. God is seen as distant. The focus is always on "then," whether past or future.

Maurice's discussion of ethics is couched in terms of a divine-human relationship, but he extends it to all human relationships. His characterization of the individual's attitude toward God is equally a characterization of the individual's attitude toward other human beings. In this light, Maurice uses words such as "conventional," "suspicious," "fearful," and "partisan" to characterize destructive ethics. Motivated by fear of punishment and expectation of reward, behavior guided by destructive ethics is also characterized by "conventional" association, where the Church is equivalent to any social club,[36] suspicion of other persons, fear, and sectarianism. Sectarianism is a good general term to describe the orientation. Exclusion is central. Persons act as atoms in a Hobbesian universe on the basis of each against all; the dominant mode of relationship is competition.

Constructive ethics begins where the liturgy begins, with the affirmation of God as Father and of human beings as God's children. Whereas to live destructive ethics is to live a lie, to live constructive ethics is to live the truth. On this point, Vaclav Havel's concept of living in truth comes to mind.[37] The pervasive emphasis on person is crucial. That God's self-revelation comes in the form of a person determines the shape of Maurice's positive discussion of ethics. In the first place, it affirms the union of Godhead and human flesh; this is the foundation of ethically responsible action, and it is the content of Maurice's Christocentrism. In the second place, this revelation of God in a person reveals that Truth is a way, a life to be lived, not a thing to be had.[38] Consequently, it results in an ethics of "style" as opposed to one of adherence to rules. The person who lives constructive ethics sees himself or herself as a child of God. S/he sees every other person in a similar light. Maurice is quite clear about this: "we forfeit our own right to Him when we fail to assert a right in Him for all [humankind]."[39] Destructive ethics is exclusive and sectarian, while constructive ethics is inclusive and universal. The one grows out of alienation and lives by fear; the other grows out of reconciliation and lives by love.

Maurice would insist that he has not constructed an ideal beyond human reach, that he has not constructed anything at all. He has pointed to a principle that lies at the root of human existence. Whether he is correct could be approached as a question of belief, or it could be approached as a question for empirical verification. Neither approach would constitute proof, and Maurice favors subordinating the theoretical question of correctness to the practical matter of living as if it were true. In other words, the real significance of the ethical vision contained in these sermons is its connection with the worship of the Church. In order to describe constructive ethics, Maurice describes the shape of the liturgy. The structure of common prayer, the mode of humankind's converse with God, is the model for humankind's own existence, for converse among persons.

This clarifies Maurice's horror at the thought that the Church of England was founded on compromise. If the form of our converse with God forms our converse with other persons, then the shape of the liturgy is the crucial moral question. The discussion of liturgy also clarifies the importance of the distinction between "worship" and "theological study." If the form of our worship forms our theological thought, then the way to correct our doctrine, to reform our perception of the world, is through the form of our worship. The liturgy starts with the union of Godhead with human flesh. Its action is at once human and divine. That is the shape Maurice seeks for all human action. The point is to recognize that "the spiritual is also the practical, that it belongs not more to the temple than to the countinghouse and the workshop."[40]

Which is to say, finally, that "liturgy" is something that we live always and everywhere, that our work as God's children is to make the world our home, a place where God and God's children can dwell.

3. Depth Theology

That understanding of liturgy at the beginning of Maurice's formal involvement with the Christian Socialist movement is complemented by an important theological work which contributed directly to the "end" of his involvement. That he dedicates *Theological Essays* to Tennyson is a warning against drawing the boundaries of theology too sharply parallel to the warning against drawing the boundaries of liturgy too close. Coleridge, Wordsworth, and Tennyson are as important to the development of Anglican theology in the nineteenth century as those who are more narrowly defined and formally trained as theologians. The voices of the first two are reflected in Maurice's insistence that "a Theology which does not correspond to the deepest thoughts and feelings of human beings cannot be a true Theology."

The "Advertisement" says that the book was written in response to a request by a "Lady, once a Member of the Society of Friends" that Maurice write a book "especially addressed to Unitarians." The search for a theology that corresponds to the deepest thoughts and feelings of human beings leads Maurice to respond to a specific request, envision a particular audience of dissenters with whom he has a long personal connection, and retain the sermonic style in which the essays were composed. He hopes to evoke "the feeling of one who is addressing actual [persons] with whom he sympathizes, not opponents with whom he is arguing." He expands on this in the preface to the second edition, where he insists that he has no ambition "to overturn radically a mature system of belief," to "unsettle" his readers "in their opinions," or bring them to his, but only "to show that God has laid a foundation" on which they "may stand together."[41]

Writing after his dismissal from King's College, which was a direct result of the initial publication of these essays, Maurice reports that he cannot "pretend that any recent experience of mine, either in a College or in the Church, has in the least changed my opinion, that our formularies are the best protection we have, against the exclusiveness and cruelty of private judgements." The fact of the Atonement, he writes, "is lost to numbers of people who are very earnest and who desire to be thoroughly Christian, through the restless efforts which their understandings make to apprehend the cause of it."[42] He writes sarcastically that he admires "those who can believe in the Love of God and can love their brethren in spite of the opinion which they seem to cherish, that He has doomed them to destruction. I am sure," he continues,

> that their faith is as much purer and stronger than mine, as it is than their own system. But if the system does prevent me from believing that which God's word, the Gospel of Christ, the witness of my own conscience, the miseries and necessities of the universe, compel me to believe, I must throw it off.[43]

Here Maurice makes two crucial distinctions, that between understanding and reason, and that between faith and system. We have met the distinction between faith and system in the *Kingdom of Christ* and the distinction between understanding and reason in discussion of Coleridge in Chapter Two. You will recall from that discussion that reason is common to all human beings and provides unmediated access to Truth. Understanding, on the other hand, is mediated by perception and therefore subject to distortion, including the distortion of sin. Maurice puts the distinctions to work in his comments on the Bible, which he calls "the Book of life." Rigid orthodoxy has turned it into a Book of Death. It is treated in a way in which no other book is treated. The divine method of it is despised; it is reduced into a collection of broken sentences; these are used in the most reckless irreverent manner by any one who has a notion of his own to defend, or a notion of an adversary to attack. The posture of students and learners towards it is abandoned by those who yet profess to accept it as their only guide and authority. There must be something very wrong in our belief, when this is our habitual practice.[44]

This leads Maurice to address the question of inspiration and raise a problem that continues to generate considerable controversy: public discourse about religion in general and the Bible in particular. He knows he can silence an objector by lapsing into purely idiosyncratic language, by signaling that he is speaking a language he cannot interpret to anyone outside his own circle. But he rejects this exclusivist approach, arguing instead that "inspired language is the most inclusive and comprehensive of all language," that "divine truth lies beneath all the imperfect forms of truth" human beings have perceived, "sustaining them, not contradicting them." If a "particular temper or habit" characterizes a person, a country, or "an age," one who believes in a revelation must "naturally conclude that there must be an affinity between this temper or habit, and some side of that Revelation"; "search earnestly for the point of contact between them"; and rejoice when that point of contact is recognized.[45] The more we look into discussions of different parties, he says, the more we find that

> however narrow and exclusive they may be, comprehension is their watchword. We separate from our fellows on the plea that they are not sufficiently comprehensive; we strive to break down fences which other people have raised, even while we are making a thicker and more thorny one ourselves.[46]

"Dogmatism," he notes,

> is not the antagonist of private judgement. The most violent assertor of his private judgement is the greatest dogmatist. And, conversely, the loudest assertor of the dogmatical authority of the Church, is very apt to be the most vehement and fanatical stickler for his own private judgements.[47]

It seems, he says, that if we start from the belief that "Charity is the ground and centre of the Universe, God is Charity," we "restore that distinctness which our Theology is said to have lost, we reconcile it with the comprehension which we are all in search of."[48]

Maurice insists that if we rest on formulas, even the best of formulas, or on the "divinest" of books rather than the living God, "our foundation will be found sandy, and will crumble under our feet."[49] Those who "have to sorrow, and suffer, and work, may accept your help in improving their outward condition, but they do not accept your creed: it is nothing to them. Atheism is their natural and necessary refuge" if the only image of God with which they are presented is that of a God who allows people to be comfortable, "who is not angry," who "wishes all to be happy, but leaves them to make each other happy as well as they can."[50] Maurice rejects this understanding of God's absence:

> you look for a better day, and a united Church:—so do I. But I want to know whether the foundation is laid on which that church is to stand, or whether it is to be laid; whether the Deliverer and Head of [hu]mankind has come or whether we are to look for another?[51]

Maurice argues for a personal concept of sin. The sinner must come to the conviction that "Evil lies not in some accidents, but in me." At that point s/he "has come unawares into a more inward circle," one that is "close, narrow, dismal," in which s/he cannot rest, out of which s/he must emerge. S/he can emerge from it only when s/he begins to say, "I have sinned against some Being,—not against society merely, not against my own nature merely, but against another to whom I was bound." The sense of sin is a "sense of solitude, isolation, distinct individual responsibility" that comes to a person when s/he "recollects" how s/he has broken the cords which bind him/her to others, by not "confessing," Maurice says in revealingly exclusive language, "that he was a brother, a son, a citizen."[52]

Maurice wants to know why we speak "in sleepy language to sleepy congregations" of a God who is willing to forgive if people repent when what they want to know is how to repent, who could absolve them, and what they had to repent of?[53] Connections with family and state, especially when stated in the exclusive terms Maurice used, are likely places to address the undeniably social dimensions of those questions. No doubt, persons who have failed to act as sons, daughters, and citizens have much to repent, as do fathers, mothers, and the State.

Throughout his work, Maurice objects to the widely held notion that poor people, working-class people "only want teaching about things on the surface." On the contrary, he says, "they are groping about the roots of things, whether we know it or not. You must meet them in their underground search, and show them the way into daylight, if you want true and brave citizens, not a community of dupes and quacks."[54] Here he turns to Job. Sin cleaves very close to him; it seems as if it were part of himself, almost as if it were himself. But his righteousness belongs to him still more entirely. However strange the paradox, it is more *himself* than even that is. He must express that conviction, he does express it, though he knows, better than anyone can tell him, how much it is at variance with what he had been thinking and saying the moment before.[55]

Job expects "that his Redeemer will stand at the latter day upon the earth. But he evidently does not rest upon an expectation. It is not what this Redeemer may be or may do hereafter he chiefly thinks of. He lives. He is with him now."[56] One who cries "till I die you shall not take my integrity from me" may be "nearest...to the root of the matter,—nearest to repentance and humiliation."[57] Maurice says that if we were consistent we would believe that God is "really answering his creature and child out of the whirlwind."[58] That would require abandoning every abstraction called "God" in favor of a person.

For Maurice, this also means abandoning exclusivity. Whatever sets us above another person is an obstacle to belief in Christ. That Maurice made this claim in the exclusive patriarchal language of his age strengthens his case against parties. He said, "Whatever sets us in any wise above our fellow-men, is an obstacle to a hearty belief in *the* Man...."[59] A party that adhered to what Maurice said would be as exclusive as any other party and as much of an obstacle to realization of the universal society. When the faith that Christ has taken the nature of every person has possessed our whole being, "exclusiveness of any kind cannot dwell with it."[60] There is not room for both Christ and exclusiveness.

Our method of defending the atonement is what has perverted it. We do not take seriously the fact that the cross destroyed sin, not just its punishment. There is "no corner of God's universe" over which God's "love has not brooded." Christ came into the world "expressly to reveal the kingdom of Heaven, and to bring us into it." Jesus and his apostles speak of this kingdom as "the kingdom of righteousness, peace, joy in the Holy Ghost. They present Righteousness, Love, Truth, to us as substantial realities, as the Nature of the Living and Eternal God..." inherited by all who claim to be made in the image of God. "And since they reveal Heaven to us, they of necessity make known Hell also. The want of Righteousness, Truth, Love, the state which is contrary to these, is and must be Hell."[61]

Because every attempt "to draw lines and limitations about the Gospel of God, for the purpose of dividing the righteous from the wicked, has tended to confound them,—to put evil for good and good for evil," Maurice pledges to "abstain in future from all such attempts," to ask whether God has "established eternal distinctions, which become clear to us when, and only when, we are content to be the heralds" of God's "free and universal love."[62]

Paul takes for granted that he is justified not because he is Saul of Tarsus, "a Hebrew of Hebrews," but because he is human. This leads Maurice to examine the human "constitution." Once we know what that constitution is, he says, "our main business" will be to ask what there is that has hindered human beings from being in conformity with it.[63]

If we desire coherent and orderly thoughts, a center must exist around which they revolve. It is "unspeakably important that we should not choose this center and so create a system for ourselves, but that we should find it. Then we may find also what are the orbits and interdependencies of the bodies which it illuminates."[64] For Maurice, that center is God. When we follow our inclinations, "when we set up to govern ourselves, and forget that there is a supernatural government established within us, we become disorganized and bestial."[65] Following Joseph Butler, Maurice insists that

> we are essentially social beings just as much as we are individuals.... I am certain that I have no self that I can love,—nay, that self must be an object of intense torment and hatred to me, unless I am the member of a body. I am certain that I cannot be the member of a body consisting of persons, unless I am myself a person; that I cannot love another person unless I do also love myself. Bring in the belief of...the one Centre of society, and that great moral contradiction is felt to be a great moral necessity; one which we can welcome and rejoice in, and act upon.[66]

Instead of "doing their utmost to exalt the Church," Maurice writes, the Apostles

> did nothing. They spoke of the Church as *in* God the Father and in Jesus Christ; they told those who belonged to it that they were created and redeemed in Christ Jesus and called; they bade them remember that they had no worth or greatness of their own; they said that they were to be witnesses...of the redemption which had been wrought out for them by the love of God through the sacrifice of Christ; they said that in proportion as they renounced idols, and devil worship, and parties, and claimed the dignity of spiritual creatures, and acted as if they were sons [and daughters] of God and members one of another, they would be such witnesses.

How could people "who *had* this position make one for themselves?" What had people "who could *exercise* such a mighty power over the world to do with asserting or vaunting it?"[67]

Maurice speaks of "a secret Manicheism" that has "been infecting the practice of the Church, while she has denounced the heresy in terms." That Manicheism will continue to gain strength until "the idea of a regenerated humanity supersedes and extinguishes it."[68] The real ascension of Christ "in the flesh" means that we do not have to ascend to heaven and "bring God down" nor plunge into the depths to bring God up. God is united with humankind, and we have to live as though we believed it.

Maurice says that Christ is present to us in the same way Christ was present to the Apostles, that "place cannot separate us." Maurice emphasizes that Christ is the judge of the living and the dead, that our popular discourses on the last judgment shift attention away from that fact to some future tribunal. But the "tribunal" is here and now. Judgment, for Maurice, is more concerned with "discrimination or discovery" than with assignment of penalties.[69] When Paul wishes to teach about Christ's coming, the word he most often uses is *apokalypsis*, "unveiling." Or he speaks of *phanerosis*, "manifestation." Each of these words "receives the greatest illustration from the Apostle's own history. Whenever he gives the story of his conversion, he describes it as an unveiling of Christ to his bodily eye; when he lays open the principle and meaning of his conversion, he represents it as the revealing or unveiling of Christ *in* him."[70] Maurice connects Paul's use of "day" (Romans 13, I Thessalonians) with the *yom Yahweh* of Hebrew Scripture.

> The 'coming' of the Apostles' Creed, and the 'coming again' of the Nicene Creed, must both indicate, if we derive our interpretation of them from Scriptures, not that Christ will resume earthly conditions, or will take a throne in some part of this earth, but that He will be manifested as He is.[71]

When speaking of the "last day," Maurice asks,

> Is it not one which has dawned on the world already, which our consciences tell us we may dwell in now, which therefore Scripture and reason both affirm must wax clearer and fuller till He who is the Sun of righteousness is felt to be shining everywhere, and till there is no corner of the universe into which his beams have not entered?[72]

Truth is not "that which every man troweth" but "that which lies at the bottom of all men's trowings, that in which those trowings have their only meeting point."[73]

"Concern about reputation," Maurice writes, "is the great hindrance to usefulness." "If we desire to be useful, we must struggle against it night and day."[74] The Bible is meant to awaken questions. A Church, instead of stifling those questions should "encounter and satisfy" them.[75] Maurice emphasizes that the "Spirit of God has come down, not on the great prophet only, but for the whole flock of Christ."[76] If we wish "to limit the movements of that Spirit which bloweth where it listeth, that we may prove ourselves to be within the circle of His influence, we offer sad evidence that we *are* resisting Him."[77] Maurice speaks of "the horrible notion of making the safety of the soul a motive for violations of Truth, nay, of making Truth merely a means to safety."[78] Individuals, Maurice says, "have fancied that Christ came, not as He said, to save the *world*, but to save *them*, that they might not be judged like their fellows."[79]

The world "contains the elements of which the Church is composed. In the Church, these elements are penetrated by a uniting, reconciling power. The Church is, therefore, human society in its normal state; the World, that same society irregular and abnormal." The world is "the Church without God... Deprive the Church of its Center, and you make it into a world."[80]

Eternity is not "a lengthening out or continuation of time." They are "generically different." If you've listened carefully to a child's questions, Maurice says, "you may often think that it knows more of eternity than of time. The succession of years confounds it; it mixes the dates which it has been instructed in most strangely; but its intuition of something which is beyond all dates makes you marvel."[81] Instead of picturing

> some future bliss, calling that eternal life, and determining the worth of it by the number of years, or centuries, or millenniums, we are bound to say once and for all: 'This is the eternal life, that which Christ has brought with Him, that which we have in Him, the knowledge of God; the entering into His mind and character, the knowing him as we only can know any person, by sympathy, fellowship, love.[82]

Unless "the Spirit of the Father and the Son were with us, we could not break loose from the fetters of Time, the confusions of Sense, the narrowness of Selfishness." If we "yield to that Spirit we can have fellowship with those who are nigh and those who are far off; with [persons] of every habit, color, opinion; with those whom the veil of flesh divides from us; with Him who is the Perfect Charity; with the Father and the Son who dwell in the Unity of one blessed and eternal Spirit."[83]

Eternal punishment consists of "being without the knowledge of God, who is love, and of Jesus Christ, who has manifested it." Eternal life consists of "having the knowledge of God and of Jesus Christ.... Eternity in relation to God has nothing to do with time or duration."[84] Maurice refers to Chrysostom's understanding of "the second death" as "the death of Sin." He also speaks favorably of Origen, whose opponents consigned him to "endless perdition because he had held the opinion that his fellow-beings were not intended for it."[85] "To govern," Maurice writes, "was the function of the Latin Church; theology was to be used as an instrument of government."[86] Luther declared that what human beings want "is freedom from sin and not freedom from punishment."[87] The crucial distinction is between seeking freedom from punishment and seeking freedom from sin. Sin, according to Maurice, is "eternal misery."

4. The Union of Godhead with Human Flesh

For Maurice, the central reality of human existence is "the union of Godhead with human flesh." Human relationships are not "artificial types of something divine," but the means "through which human beings ascend to any knowledge of the divine." Every broken human relationship is "a violation of the higher law," a "hindrance and a barrier to the perception of that higher law," a veil drawn between the spirit of humankind and humankind's God.[88] Maurice's understanding of the incarnation places the relationship of God and humankind at the center of existence, but it does so in such a way as to focus attention on human relationship as a concrete observable reality rather than on God as an abstract principle or concept.

Although Maurice's appropriation of the incarnation as a symbol had a marked effect on his perception of God that is crucial for theology, it is at the same time an anthropologically significant appropriation. The perception of God through the union of Godhead with human flesh shifts human relationships to center stage.

That Maurice was willing to accept the radical implications of this shift is evinced in his preface to *Moral and Metaphysical Philosophy*, where, in referring to the voice of God, he affirms that "a *vox humana*, no doubt, any one must be" which reaches human ears. "And a voice which commands every one to seek the good of others more than his [or her] own, must be very human indeed. It can be no metaphysical abstraction: it must be living and personal, otherwise it can have no 'positive' result."[89] This implies, first, that, as Maurice asserts in the same preface, there is no "irreligious" truth. He not only calls any separation between Christianity and civilization into question but also grounds freedom for inquiry on the conviction that the Word is always at work in the world. Second, as a direct consequence, that there is no "irreligious" truth means that the study of concrete human relationships is the proper function of theology. The paradox that would result from God as an absolute, transcendent starting-point dissolves in the union of God with humankind. The study of human relationships admits no absolute starting-point, and it necessarily involves an approach that is structural and dynamic. Remember that Maurice cautioned against the kind of closure that would result from an allegedly complete perception of reality by divorcing himself from systems and parties that would purport to be homes but which would, in reality, be prisons.

Setting out from an incarnational base that makes an absolute starting-point a practical impossibility, Maurice undertakes to analyze human relationships and to understand their practical significance for human character, to focus not on specific acts or specific ideas but on relationships as bases for action and thought.

The shape this inquiry took after his public involvement with Christian Socialism and the Workingmen's College emerges most clearly in two series of lectures, *The Conscience* and *Social Morality*, delivered while he was professor of casuistry and moral philosophy at Cambridge.[90]

Maurice begins *The Conscience* by addressing what he calls grave doubts as to "whether the student of morals has any real subject to treat of."[91] Those doubts are answered by means of a survey which reveals that the most diverse disciplines all concern an "I" in one way or another but that none of them treat it as the proper subject matter of their inquiries. That "I" the moralist claims for his or her investigation.

Maurice insists that this starting point is concrete rather than abstract. In a general sense, "if the moral teacher adopts the distinction sanctioned by one of the ablest and most accomplished" of moral teachers by saying that s/he is concerned "with what ought to be," while "other students" are concerned "with what is, can there be a clearer or fuller confession" that s/he "means to leave the actual world for some other world" which s/he has "imagined?"[92] But Maurice never meant to leave the actual world. The moralist can speak of "Individuality" or "Personality" instead of "I." Then "the word 'I' will vanish out of his [or her] school dialect, whilst s/he is resorting to it every hour, almost every minute, if s/he is speaking" not as an academic but as a human being. "So the link between the two characters is broken." The moralist speaks of human beings, but what is most characteristic of human beings is gone: "you have killed him that you may dissect him."[93]

The point is to begin in the actual world with living persons. To do that, Maurice begins with the "I." That this does not make his approach simply an individual one is attested by the fact that he saw the word "I" not as a thing or an abstraction: "The word I, with its property of being demanded by a whole community, and yet capable of denoting a single unit, is a key to that mystery in words which makes them interpreters of the life of individuals, of nations, of ages; the discoverers of that which we have in common, the witness" of that in each person which s/he "cannot impart," which others "may guess at, but which they will never know."[94] Thus the starting point is actual and it is living. It is individual and it is communal. It is not an abstraction or a thing but a complex relationship of relationships.

Maurice defines the "I" in his discussion of the conscience, which is at once the reality that "binds the different parts of my existence together" and that "assures me that the past still belongs to me."[95] This "I" is the center of integration of individual existence. It is also intrinsically connected with the "ought." The "I" is not only the center of individual integration but also the point of contact between individual and society. It reveals that "there is an Order in which I am placed, a real order, not an imaginary one, not an order which might be desirable but which exists."[96] In other words, Maurice starts with the "I" precisely because and insofar as it represents the actual world of living persons as individual and social beings. It avoids the abstract idea of "Society" without denying the social structure of human existence.

This starting point leads Maurice to insist that rules of the conscience will never settle cases of conscience, that "rules are unfavorable to goodness and earnestness, and are not helpful in practice."[97] "The relations," he writes, "must be closer" to the person "than the rules can ever be; if [she or he] makes them dependent upon rules [she or] he renounces them."[98]

Maurice's assertion of the primacy of human relationship is demonstrated concretely in his discussion of slavery in the United States. He describes it as a condition in which "a Society has organized itself on the ground of *Property*." Slave owners are "*possessors*" and as such are "bound to each other"; slaves, on the other hand, are "*possessions*." "The Society has taught its members to look upon each other in this light, to fraternise on this ground." The discovery that the slave is also a human being and that the slave owner therefore stands in relation to him/her affects the slave owner as much as the slave: "Are there not *relations* between those who have called themselves the superior race? Are not these Relations a deeper ground of Society than Property can ever be?" By acknowledging the humanity "of the black they obtain a new conception of their own."[99] The realization of relationship undermines society based on property or rule.

Maurice's movement from casuistry to social morality is signaled near the end of *The Conscience* where he writes, "You cannot contemplate the individual [person] out of Society." But you must vindicate the position of persons

> in order that you may shew what Society is; of what it consists. If it does not consist of I's, of Persons, the Moralist has no concern with it. If it does consist of I's, of Persons, begin with asserting that character for it, then go on to investigate the relations in which the members of it stand to each other. That means, as I conceive, when translated into the book speech, 'Begin with Casuistry; go on to Moral Philosophy. First make it clear what you mean by a Person; that you will do when you make it clear what you mean by a Conscience; then treat these Persons as if they did form real bodies, and tell us out of history, not out of your own fancy, what these bodies are.[100]

Investigation begins with the recognition of the individual's existence in society. It takes both the individual's existence and society seriously and proceeds by examining their interrelationship. As Maurice suggested, the "soundest Moral

Science will be that which is demanded by the necessities of Practical Politics."[101] The analysis begins in the actual world with living persons, then moves toward a practical (not technical or artificial) moral science that is at the same time a political reality.

The separation between casuistry and moral philosophy is not airtight; both are present from the beginning. But the movement into explicit treatment of the second area (in *Social Morality*) is significant in two respects. In the first place, it provides an occasion for Maurice to acknowledge that he found the effort to make moral theology a distinct subject impractical; "it must be so for anyone who discovers beneath the Conscience which testifies of our personal existence, beneath all the order of human Society, a divine foundation."[102] In the second place, the movement into social morality prompts Maurice to state his method in terms of criticism of Christianity on the basis of belief in Christ.

More generally, this is the method we encountered in *The Kingdom of Christ*, where system was distinguished from principle. System, like rule and exchange, is subject to criticism on the basis of relationship. That Christ is understood in terms of relationship is critical for this method. Given Maurice's conception of the incarnation, Christ implies the union of Godhead with human flesh and a person in relation with other persons. That Christ is understood in terms of relationship simultaneously shifts human relationship to center stage and perceives such relationships in terms of an "I" which is individual and communal. The shift provides the occasion for an explicit statement of the individual-social starting point of ethics.

By placing the radical paradox of the eternal in time, the union of Godhead with human flesh, at the center of existence, Maurice makes clear that the problem is not a matter of observation but of action; existence is the problem. The concern of the ethical is with existence, with what Kierkegaard labels "becoming subjective."

No fixed point, no static base exists on which to build an ethical or scientific edifice. To the extent that a fixed point is found, it is a delusion resulting from the transformation of a process into a product. As Kierkegaard noted, this is like sitting in the back seat of a speeding carriage trying to stop it by holding tightly to the seat in front of us.[103] No Archimedean point exists outside of time; the base, the superstructure, and the acting subject are all in process. Where existence is the problem, process is its very nature; to see it in fixed or static terms is to misunderstand it.

Four

THE FEVER OF THE MISCELLANEOUS MAN

Maurice developed his theory of adult education most clearly in a series of six lectures delivered in 1854 to announce the formation of a Working Men's College in North London. The immediate backdrop for the lectures is Maurice's dismissal from King's College as a direct result of the controversy generated by his *Theological Essays*. More generally, though, as the dedication of the published lectures to John Ludlow confirms, the deeper background is the whole period of Maurice's involvement, beginning in 1848, with the Christian Socialist movement.

The dedication traces that movement's origins to a letter from Ludlow describing contemporary events in Paris. The letter riveted Maurice's attention on the superficiality of the material civilization promoted in France by Louis Philippe and on the duty of British clergy to resist the growing fascination of the British working class with that civilization. Events of 1848 crystallized Maurice's vision of a contest between "material" and "Christian" civilization, between a civilization based on selfishness and accumulation and one that "does not make the accumulation of material treasures or the increase of material enjoyments its main objects."

1. The Shape of the City Itself

When Maurice confronted the events of 1848, civilization, the shape of the city itself, was the question.

Maurice delivered the lectures in the West-End of London, to an audience that included everyone except the working class. He was, obviously, not a working-class theorist. His involvement with socialism is often read as a middle-class reaction against a threat posed by an increasingly organized and politicized British working class, holy water to soothe middle-class heartburn.

In a sense, Maurice is speaking to himself in these lectures, distilling six years of socialist involvement into an educational scheme. The dedication to Ludlow suggests a sense in which he is speaking to a professional audience that (in the person of Ludlow) has shared this involvement from the beginning. He is also speaking to an educated West London audience that has not shared this involvement, certainly not to the same extent or in the same way as Ludlow.

Maurice states in the last lecture that he is not making a public appeal soliciting funds. But he is making a collection, collecting himself, collecting the "movement," and collecting the "educated" class (Coleridge's clerisy) for a conversation with workers, an experiment in civilization.

The series begins with two questions: (1) "Historically, did adult education or education of children come first?" and (2) "Is leisure or work the natural ally of learning?"[1] Both questions grow out of familiar class-specific objections to proposals for educational programs intended for adult workers, and they indicate the depth of Maurice's familiarity with his audience.

The first question grows out of a widely shared assumption that educational programs for adults are entirely dependent on educational programs for children. If children are not properly educated, adult education is always too little too late. This barely veils a pair of assumptions that Maurice challenges in his first two lectures: that education is exclusively for children (a nineteenth-century version of "everything I need to know I learned in kindergarten"), and that education can take place only where one is relieved of the responsibility of work.

The assumptions are so closely related that the second often presents itself as a variant of the first: education is what happens in school, and, by the time one is an adult, it is too late for that. But the second may also take a more class-biased form: adult education is limited to those who have the luxury of leisure, because workers (and serious business-people) do not have time. The immediate effect of these assumptions is to make adult education either infantile or elitist.

Maurice's first lecture is a refutation of the claim that education of children takes historical precedence. Education of children did not, he argues, come first in Britain, and that is not a weakness but a strength.

That Maurice sees the Working Men's College as an experiment in civilization is reflected in the creative tension of his genealogy, fed by two streams, Latin and Saxon. For Maurice, both streams have a "Christian" base in that they direct the scholar's attention to two worlds that s/he inhabits simultaneously, one spiritual, one physical. The first form of the Latin stream, the monastic tradition, was open to rich and poor on the condition that they devote themselves to a new life, the life of the scholar, turned from the physical toward the spiritual world. This tradition is exemplified in Alcuin's educational program for Charlemagne, by which monasticism's spiritual and scholarly turn is kept in close contact with the everyday physical involvement of practical politics. This form is distorted when neglect of the physical leads to its denial or when withdrawal from the world results in complete separation. Saxon education, exemplified in King Alfred, is a corrective. He was, Maurice reports, immersed first in practical affairs and "local" lore, not exposed to Latin learning at all until he was twelve, and then only in translation.

Two tensions are at work in this genealogy. The most explicit is one of orientation, which is much like that described in discussion of Coleridge in

Chapter Two above. The Latin and Saxon streams work when they make the scholar aware of living toward a spiritual world, in a material one. They fail when they split those worlds and divide their students between them. Only slightly less explicit is a tension between location and language. The Saxon stream flows opposite the Latin, from "local" toward "global" language. Both streams work when they make their students at home. They fail when they render their students permanently homeless. For Maurice, this permanent homelessness is an imprisonment most antagonistic to freedom and order, and therefore most antithetical to the aims of education.

Maurice continues his genealogy with a second form of the Latin stream, Norman education associated with the eleventh-century invasion of England by William the Conqueror, which reasserts monastic education in the face of Saxon localism. Because this reassertion is associated with conquest, it introduces an elitist character into the Latin stream. This elitism is intimately connected with issues of language and location that developed in England under the influence, first, of the domination of universities by the mendicant orders (Franciscans and Dominicans) and, second, under the influence of Wycliffe.

The universities that emerged in the twelfth century identified learning with the Latin stream reasserted in the Norman conquest but rooted via Boethius in Rome. Maurice associates the Scholastic separation of "facts" and "words" that took place in universities dominated by the mendicant orders with debates around language and locality identified in England with Wycliffe. In this regard, Maurice notes the emergence of colleges in the thirteenth and fourteenth centuries as "local" alternatives to the mendicants. A college is a community defined not only by its relationship to the university's circle of knowledge but also by its members and their location in a particular place.

Wycliffe's concern with language, entangled with the formation of colleges, leads under the influence of the reformations of the sixteenth century to an interest in philology. Coupled with formation of boys' schools (such as Eton) in association with particular colleges, this concern with language gives rise to the grammar schools that dominate education of children by the time Maurice writes.

By the seventeenth century, the separation of practical wisdom from colleges and universities is pronounced and growing. The schools and the world are no longer separate spheres but competing realms, the schools concerned with the education of gentlemen conversant in the Latin tradition, while the world is concerned increasingly with practicality and productivity. The result, Maurice says, was a practical emphasis outside the universities on educational schemes to produce "hands, not men."

Maurice sees a reciprocal influence between adult and "infant" education, related to his claim that all education should be education for adulthood. The zeal for infant education has two values: first, the encounter with a child is undeniably an encounter with a person, not a machine. Emphasis on the child directs attention to persons because it cannot be initially concerned exclusively with reading, writing, and ciphering. Second, concern with infant education directs attention to adult education insofar as it demands attention to the teaching of teachers.

2. Learning and Working

In the second lecture, Maurice turns to the connection between learning and working. Though the grammar school is derivative historically from the College, it had increasingly come to take priority until English Universities were transformed into little more than advanced grammar schools. From the beginning, Maurice has insisted on the danger posed by the reversal and the resulting separation. In the first place, it is impossible to keep children in schools that have no connection with their world, both because the world is more exciting and because the world of work is able to offer larger bribes than any school to both parents and children.

The supposed separation of learning and working denies the experience of workers. Maurice insists that adults who have been at work in the world have been learning, even if the awareness of their learning has been sporadic and undisciplined.

Maurice develops two arguments for the connection of learning with working. The first notes the extent to which play is serious work. A human inclination toward work is evident not only in adults but also in children. Education that holds the attention of children or adults has to take into account the level of commitment to disciplined activity reflected in children's play as much as in adult's work. The second is an historical account related to the genealogy developed in his first lecture. The monastic tradition in which he located the origins of British education was rooted through Benedict in work. Maurice points to a rhythm of work and rest characteristic of the Benedictine rule that is more properly a rhythm of physical and intellectual work that explicitly connects the two worlds of which Maurice and Coleridge speak.

Referring to the genealogy of his first lecture, Maurice notes a tension between monastic and popular learning. If either had come to totally dominate, he says, it would have destroyed the nation in the process of destroying the other. The rhythm of monastic and popular learning grounded national development. Labor and learning both give birth to leisure, which threatens to murder its parents, as illustrated by the excesses of Scholasticism. The Reformation reaction to Scholasticism, at its best, connected faith and learning with ordinary work, and in that sense claimed the spirit of Benedictine monasticism for ordinary people. This is exemplified for Maurice in the Elizabethan Age, in which work and literature blossomed. As a representative of that age, Shakespeare is not an exceptional case so much as a model for adult education:

> instead of setting him up as a mere marvellous phenomenon and an excuse for our self-worship, it might surely be better to ask whether he does not give us the hint of a cultivation at once popular and profound, humane and national, which might be available for thousands, who are not separated from their fellows by any accident of class or condition.[2]

Maurice's target, as he points out at the beginning of the third lecture, is not work but "bustling" and what he calls "the fever of the miscellaneous man."

In his reflections on the connection between learning and working, Maurice consistently returns to what he sees as a natural desire to discover connections beneath the miscellany of everyday work. To this natural tendency, he attributes a widespread interest in mathematics among those involved in mechanical labor. Pointing to biographies of well-known success stories, such as Richard Arkwright, Maurice notes a contrary tendency on the part of readers to be so dazzled by combinations and effects, especially the accumulation of capital, that we forget the discoveries and struggles "in the man himself" to "understand his own meaning." But it is precisely the discoveries and struggles to understand one's own meaning that matter. Because the human soul is more precious than the spinning-jenny, the steps that lead to invention are more wonderful and more worthy of attention than the material results, whether the machine or the accumulation of capital it makes possible. The steps are there in every laborer, and bringing the laborer to awareness of those steps is more valuable "than all the cotton that shall be produced while the world lasts."[3]

Awareness of those steps carries with it awareness that the enemy of learning is not work, but restlessness, which is perfectly compatible and more often than not associated with leisure. Both rest and work are necessarily connected with learning, but leisure and idleness are not.

Education that works, Maurice insists, has historically led to perception of two kingdoms,

> one of which is meant for us just as much as the other. How to bring them together, how to hinder them from clashing and interfering with each other, was a great problem, *the* great problem of all. But each was always confessed to be necessary to the other; and there was a secret assurance that if it was so, they could not be confined to two different sets of subjects; that the same man must at the same time be a citizen of both, and that it was his mistake, not the mistake of the order in which he was placed, if there was any divided allegiance, any opposition of interests.[4]

Maurice was no "democrat" in the usual sense of that term, but he is opposed to a two-track system of education. All education is for human adulthood, and it is equally the right of all human beings. Coupled with this anti-classist conviction is a repudiation of the reactionary idealization of the past. "We are under no obligation whatever" to tell workers "that the former days were better than these." We might well make a case that these days are better because they have expanded facilities for work and learning, but only if we consistently regard every person "as capable of receiving a wisdom that cannot be gotten for gold, and which the gold and the crystal cannot equal."[5]

But, Maurice says, we have often done the reverse, leading workers to believe that wisdom can be gotten for gold and reducing education to a means for the acquisition of wealth. One of the results is a transformation of learning and working into "a feverish effort to produce quickly that which may look well, and be puffed largely, and be sold at a low rate, to the great loss of the purchaser."[6]

Steady work is most favorable to education, but unsteady work, "gambling work," is "the most fatal obstacle to it." Maurice said that nineteenth-century Britain was becoming "a nation of gamblers":

> We do not ask what we are to do, but what is likely to turn up, if we make such and such a cast. Handicrafts, Trades, Professions, are to be undertaken upon a calculation of chances, not from a sense of vocation. How can we think quietly, how can we pursue science, which only converses with that which *is*, while our whole minds are busy with possibilities and contingencies?[7]

Maurice summarizes his case in three points: (1) the disease that is infecting the working class is infecting all classes, (2) the disease is rooted in a habit of mind "communicated from the higher classes to the working classes," and (3) the best way of restoring the whole society is by doing what we can to reform this portion of it. Given Maurice's audience, the third point is double-edged. This is a call to the "educated" class to change its habit of mind in communication with a working class equally entitled to fully human consideration.

3. A Practice of Freedom

The diseased habit of mind that Maurice attributes to educated and working classes is a confusion developed in his lectures inaugurating the Working Men's College as in his later lectures at Cambridge with reference to a pervasive confusion between person and thing. That confusion, associated with the illusion that money is the measure of human worth, threatens to turn workers into serfs, to undermine freedom, civilization, and commerce.

Maurice's experiment in civilization depends on a practice of freedom that is intimately connected with the affirmation of persons. The very possibility of civilization requires a transformation not of one class but of the whole society: "the reformation must begin at both ends...we must raise Work to make it fit for association with Learning, as well as bring Learning to bear upon Work."[8]

Civilization as transformation of the whole society connects education with freedom and order. In his fourth lecture, Maurice connects this with a "mystical" dimension that he finds in the attraction of music education for workers. Music, like mathematics, has no obvious utility for already overburdened workers. The attraction of both, Maurice suggests, lies in their connection with order and with a capacity in the present to look before and after, which he associates with memory and hope. Education for adulthood, whether it is designed for children or for adults, is intimately connected with the discipline of creative work. Contrary to the claim that education is antithetical to work, Maurice finds considerable evidence for a human orientation toward work that is connected with desire for order and reflected in the interpenetration of freedom and discipline. The absence of discipline is not freedom but bustling superficiality and busyness.

In keeping with the three "rules" he outlines near the end of the fourth lecture, Maurice moves from careful consideration of the objects (or aims) of education and "the tempers of those we would guide," which occupied his attention in the first four lectures, to consideration in the last two lectures of the studies and teachers in a Working College. In every step along the way, he borrows freely from his predecessors.

Maurice's description emphasizes interdisciplinarity in the formation of a college that is a community of learners and workers. Though the fifth lecture is primarily concerned with the studies and the sixth with the teachers, it is not possible to separate discussion of studies from discussion of teachers. The interdisciplinarity of the place is embodied in the teachers more than in the range of subjects studied. In his description of subjects, Maurice insists on a movement back from the present into the past, from politics into history, a movement in which teachers and students are passionately engaged. The point at every step along the way is for teachers and students to be fully present to one another in community. He moves from history into geography, from geography into ethics. In each case, the teacher is to make a particular study the means of illustrating and cultivating the method which belongs to all studies. Subject matters are not neglected, but method is the "permanence" that lies behind all of them. Like Coleridge, Maurice evokes the permanence of thought and words exhibited in history. If freedom and order are the ends of education, they are to be achieved not in the particularities of subject matters but in the discipline to see through all of them. "What we want," Maurice says, speaking specifically of Ethics, but referring to all the other subjects as well, "is not to put things into our pupils' minds, so much as to set in order what we find there, to untie knots, to disentangle complicated threads."[9] The movement is always from subject matter to principle, from present to past, always in conversation between persons fully engaged in the world. Each subject is an entrance into all subjects. Completing the list, Maurice moves from ethics to poetry, art, logic, language (with emphasis in English on etymology), physiology and health, mathematics, philosophy, and theology. The studies in a Working College are not defined primarily by subject matter but by the encounter of students and teachers who are both working and learning. Wholeness is communicated not by a "complete" range of subject matters but by a range of subjects, each of which serves as an entry into a community of scholars.

Whatever tends to make a person more human, Maurice says, is part of education. He attends in his final lecture to "amusements" and to the relationship between "high" and "popular" culture. His high sacramental view of history is repeated here in the assertion that "history is the voice of God."[10] More modestly, it is the place where human beings encounter God's voice, and the task of the teacher is to cultivate disciplines for hearing that voice through the multiplicities of the world.

Much of the last lecture is devoted to what looks like an elimination of funding possibilities, what Maurice insists is a clearing of ground. He argues against a public appeal because of the fleetingness of public support. Expand and correct the public mind, he admonished in the first lecture, do not stoop to it. He argues against government funding while acknowledging a role for government in certification and accreditation. Governments should insure that professors are delivering what they profess wherever they profess it. In a departure from a position he had developed earlier in his career, he argues against church support as well as support from the Universities, societies, sects, or a special "Order" for educators. What Maurice describes in the end is a "club" that is a community of scholars engaged in a neighborhood experiment, teachers who are tutors, not professors, who give lessons, not lectures.

4. Time, Social Theory, and Educational Practice

If this is nothing more than holy water for middle-class heartburn, then Maurice's dismissal from King's College was either a grave injustice or a profound misunderstanding. Dispensation of such holy water would presumably have served the conservative interests of Maurice's accusers and been a source of comfort to the college administration. But his accusers were more perceptive than disciples who in retrospect rendered him harmless at best, forgettably muddled at worst.

The immediate cause of his dismissal was an understanding of time articulated in *Theological Essays* with reference to eternal punishment. But there can be little doubt that five years of Christian Socialism was a contributing factor. The result was the Working Men's College, which stands alongside the *Theological Essays* as the embodiment of Maurice's mature theology. That theology, articulated not only in metaphysical speculation on the nature of time but also in the development of social theory into educational practice, did more to cause than to cure the heartburn of his critics.

The historiography of Christian Socialism, more than its history, sheds some light on the discrepancy between these widely divergent assessments, as holy water to soothe heartburn or as fuel to ignite it.

Ralph Pugh describes three schools in that historiography: (1) social ethics (dominant from 1880 through 1920), (2) Christian theology (dominant from 1920 through 1950), and (3) political liberalism (dominant since 1950). The first two focus on Maurice, the third on Ludlow. Historians of social ethics have depicted Christian Socialism as "a scheme of working-class amelioration" in which "the Christian faith was important only as a moral impulse for the furtherance of the social agenda." They have depicted Maurice as a moralist whose theology was "murky" and "ultimately irrelevant," whose movement was relevant politically only for its alliance with labor and socialism, both of which quickly left it behind. With the Maurice revival from 1920 through 1950, a second historiographical school emerged that appreciated Maurice as a theologian. This school has depicted Christian Socialism as "a theological reformation" directed particularly to an "atheistic social revolution" and an "anti-social evangelical" one. Political liberalism has embraced Ludlow's claim to be the true founder of the movement and generally depicted Maurice as "muddle-headed and/or innately conservative on social issues." This last school has emphasized the movement's roots, via Ludlow, in French socialism, thereby highlighting a genealogical and ideological divergence from Marxism.

Both the first and third schools have effectively jettisoned Maurice's theology in the process of subsuming Christian Socialism into a broad movement of political liberalism quite distinct from any radical variant of socialism. In the process, they have gone beyond Marx's dismissal and abandoned what Maurice took to be the most essential aspect of his thought, the digging characteristic of theology. The best one can hope for without digging is an impressive building with no foundation.

That is not even holy water. Given this understanding, it is hardly surprising when G.D.H. Cole depicts Christian Socialism as "no more than a ripple on the surface of a country on which the sun of economic advance was shining with a deep, though murky, light,"[11] or when Edward Norman depicts it as politically naive, disconnected from "scientific" socialism.

But in spite of himself, Norman picks up a crucial element of Maurice's thought, the element that probably most exacerbated the heartburn of critics and allies alike, when he speaks of Maurice's "desire to purge the Christian world of wrong attributes through the construction of a screen of analytical interpretation that did not itself become a theoretical system."[12]

Recall that Coleridge collapsed metaphysical into epistemological concerns and folded an ethical dimension into the mix as well. This is the explosive mixture that Maurice inherited and that Mill perceptively recognized as an alternative to Toryism as well as to Benthamism. Norman sees "no thread of continuity" between Maurice's early political radicalism and later Christian Socialism. In this he follows Torben Christensen, but the intersecting genealogies and narratives developed in the first three chapters of this book suggest otherwise. The theologians may have failed to produce narrative histories, but they encountered Maurice at the core of his work. The thread is a radical commitment to human existence grounded in a divine reality that embodies freedom and order. It is woven through Maurice's work in the development of an educational practice directed entirely to enabling an expanding circle of friends to perceive and to act on that ground.

Like Coleridge, Maurice moved away from political journalism because of its superficiality. Both thinkers were driven by a concern with the inward, but also with the depths. Ignorance of the depths contributed to a remarkably successful English culture of containment. Martin Wiener's influential analysis describes this as a cultural containment of industrial capitalism by the growth of the professional class between 1850 and 1980. This explains, he says, a "decline of the industrial spirit" that accounts for Britain's loss of industrial superiority in spite of the considerable head start it enjoyed in industrialization. But it is also a cultural containment of socialism critical to interpretation of Maurice.

As a professor at King's College, Maurice played a significant role in socializing young men into a growing professional class, particularly in the preparation of young men for ordination in the Anglican Church. If his dismissal from that position was not misguided, it would suggest a failure on his part to fulfill that role. This is precisely what gives his educational theory revolutionary potential. He spoke to a "professional" class, not to enlarge it but to enlist it.

The question is to enlist it in what.

Ralph Pugh's historians of social ethics and political liberalism have, with Martin Wiener, relegated Maurice to the role of fence builder. It would be difficult to dispute that characterization of his role if he had not been dismissed from King's College. But the dismissal suggests that he was, at the least, a poor fence builder. And the digging of the lectures threatens to undermine the fence altogether.

That is the point. An alliance between the intelligentsia and the workers had revolutionary potential for socialism in Britain. Socialism was sidetracked by a remarkably effective containment culture working on two fronts, an ameliorative front that slowed the growth of industrial capitalism and gave it in Britain, if not a human, then at least a less monstrous face; and a defensive front that successfully fended off the socialist specter that haunted Europe in 1848.

Five

CONCLUSION

An essay, neither the first word nor the last, is by definition not only exploratory but also incomplete. It ends, as it begins, with unanswered questions.

This essay began with philosophical and theological questions about economic language, specifically the language of efficiency, productivity, and Market mechanisms that has come to contain speculation on human being, human action, and human reason. Those questions guided the essay into a territory defined by space (focusing on Britain), time (focusing on the nineteenth century), and persons (focusing on F.D. Maurice and Samuel Taylor Coleridge).

The questions with which it ends are also philosophical and theological, and they direct attention to further historical investigation and to further reflection on language as it relates to being and acting in the world.

The most immediate question, with which the previous chapter ended, concerns the relationship between intelligentsia and workers. The claim that this relationship was sidetracked is a comment on its containment that suggests an area for further historical research. Fabian socialism, for example, was intensely concerned with that relationship, and immensely influential in the formation of the British (and Swedish) Welfare States of the twentieth century as well as the rise and transformation of the British Labour Party. Tracing the arc of British socialism from the middle of the nineteenth century through Fabianism to the New Labour Party should provide substantial insight into the process of containment. The rise of Capital, the development of labor, and the curious conflation of "pragmatism" with anti-intellectualism and evangelicalism in the United States is a closely related theme. Variations can be generated by shifting territorial as well as temporal focus. The intelligentsia in Central Europe, for example, played a major role in the "Velvet Revolutions" of the late 1980s. The relationships of those revolutions and the intelligentsia with both workers and socialisms is a richly complicated, rapidly changing, and inadequately mapped territory.

The more pervasive philosophical and theological question posed by Maurice's reading of Coleridge and his reading of history digs through the relationship of discrete classes to the activity that is essential to both. Maurice (like Marx) locates human being in action: *work* is essential to being human. Like Coleridge, he draws on explicitly Christian (and Trinitarian) language to connect work with *word*. In making this connection, Coleridge and Maurice drink from an ancient well common to Christianity and Platonism.

That they drink from an ancient well explains the rhetorical strategies that have most effectively contained them. They are branded reactionary, then embraced by defenders of the *status quo*; rejected by revolutionaries who have no use for the past; or (most effectively in the case of Maurice) split in two by reformers who isolate their political activity from its philosophical and theological sources.

Keeping work and word together in persons is revolutionary because, as Maurice noted in his sermons on the *Book of Common Prayer*, it leaves no room for exclusion. The message to the intelligentsia is clear: we are workers because we are human. If we devote ourselves to maintaining structures that deny this identity, we contribute to our own dehumanization. That is a practical rule by which to judge not only schools but also other institutions that contribute to social order by placing people in a settled society.

In their most famous and most widely read work, written at the same moment and in the same place Maurice and his colleagues were launching Christian Socialism, Marx and Engels issued a memorable call for unity among the world's workers: "Workers of the world unite! You have nothing to lose but your chains."

The clarity with which this call identified what workers had to lose in the middle of Britain's Industrial Revolution is one of its greatest strengths, a key to its influence in the more than 150 years since it was issued, and an essential ingredient of its continuing significance.

Equally significant is the fact that this crystalline call came at the end of a complex (and therefore less easily remembered) argument in which Christian Socialism was dismissed as holy water for the burning conscience of the bourgeoisie.

The dismissal was a hint taken up by ameliorative socialism, which, by effectively transforming itself into a "third way," gave Capitalism a human face, turned it into a warm global god, and complicated chains beyond recognition.

Workers—particularly the "knowledge workers" characteristic of economies more dependent on information and communication than industrial production—are seldom bound by anything so obvious as chains. We are bound by webs of work in which our products are labyrinths of closets made doubly effective by the comfort and protection they afford.

Maurice and Coleridge are important allies if we are to avoid losing our selves entirely in such comfortable labyrinths. The alternative to institutions that contribute to social order by placing people in a settled society is displacing and unsettling. Like those "true levellers" mentioned in Chapter One, we are going to have to dig in public places toward our humanity—not to make it out of nothing or to make nothing of it, but to let it grow in carefully cultivated common ground.

NOTES

Chapter 1

1. *The Life of Frederick Denison Maurice, Chiefly Told in His Own Letters.* Edited by Frederick Maurice (London: Macmillan, 1884), Vol. 1, p. 3.
2. *Ibid.*, p. 6.
3. See Williston Walker, *A History of the Christian Church* (New York: Scribner, 1970).
4. *Life*, Vol. 1, p. 7.
5. *Ibid.*, p. 9.
6. *Ibid.*, p. 20.
7. *Ibid.*
8. *Ibid.*, p. 23.
9. *Ibid.*, p. 33.
10. Max Beer, *A History of British Socialism* (New York: Arno Press, 1979), Vol. 1, p. 60.
11. Quoted in Ralph Pugh, *The Constitutive Principles of Early Victorian Christian Socialism, 1848-1854* (Ph.D. Dissertation, University of Chicago, 1994), Vol. 1, p. 51.
12. Stanley Pierson, *Marxism and the Origins of British Socialism: The Struggle for a New Consciousness* (Ithaca, N.Y.: Cornell University Press), p. 8.

Chapter 2

1. Samuel Taylor Coleridge, *Biographia Literaria, or, biographical sketches of my literary life and opinions. The Collected Works of Samuel Taylor Coleridge.* Ed. James Engell and W. Jackson Bate (Princeton, N.J.: Princeton University Press, 1983 [1817]), Vol. 7, Part 2, p. 237.
2. *Ibid.*, Vol. 7, Part 1, p. 5.
3. *Ibid.*, p. 3.
4. *Ibid.*, p. 22.
5. *Ibid.*, p. 89.
6. *Ibid.*, p. 97n.
7. *Ibid.*, p. 111.
8. *Ibid.*, pp. 117, 118.
9. *Ibid.*, p. 120.
10. *Ibid.*, p. 127.
11. *Ibid.*, p. 134.
12. *Ibid.*, p. 137.
13. *Ibid.*, p. 141.
14. *Ibid.*, p. 242.
15. *Ibid.*, p. 247.
16. *Ibid.* Translated from Coleridge's French.

17. *Ibid.*, p. 252.
18. *Ibid.*, pp. 252-255.
19. *Ibid.*, p. 304.
20. *Ibid.*, p. 305.
21. *Ibid.*, Vol. 7, Part 2, p. 5.
22. *Ibid.*, p. 13.
23. *Ibid.*, p. 12.
24. *Ibid.*, p. 13.
25. *Ibid.*, pp. 15, 16.
26. Samuel Taylor Coleridge. *Aids to Reflection. The Collected Works of Samuel Taylor Coleridge.* Ed. John Beer (Princeton, N.J.: Princeton University Press, 1993 [1825]), Vol. 9, pp. 6, 7.
27. *Ibid.*, p. 8.
28. *Ibid.*
29. *Ibid.*
30. *Ibid.*, p. 229.
31. *Ibid.*, p. 182.
32. *Ibid.*, p. 207.
33. *Ibid.*, p. 232.
34. See, for example, John H. Muirhead, *Coleridge as Philosopher* (New York: Macmillan, 1930), and Mary Ann Perkins, *Coleridge's Philosophy: The Logos as Unifying Principle* (London: Oxford University Press, 1994).

Chapter 3

1. *The Life of Frederick Denison Maurice, Chiefly Told in His Own Letters.* Edited by Frederick Maurice (London: Macmillan, 1884), Vol. 1, pp. 210-222.
2. F. D. Maurice, *The Kingdom of Christ* (London: James Clarke, 1959), Vol. 1, p. 17.
3. *Ibid.*, p. 259.
4. *Ibid.*, pp. 213, 214.
5. *Ibid.*, p. 77.
6. *Ibid.*, p. 213.
7. *Ibid.*, pp. 217, 218.
8. *Ibid.*, p. 219.
9. *Ibid.*, p. 213.
10. *Ibid.*, p. 219.
11. *Ibid.*, p. 223.
12. *Ibid.*
13. *Ibid.*, p. 238.
14. *Ibid.*, p. 240.
15. *Ibid.*, p. 245.
16. *Ibid.*, pp. 261, 262.
17. *Ibid.*, p. 262.
18. *Ibid.*

19. *Ibid.*, p. 264.
20. *Ibid.*, pp. 264, 265.
21. *Ibid.*, Vol. 2, p. 44.
22. *Ibid.*, p. 45.
23. *Ibid.*, pp. 45-47.
24. *Ibid.*, p. 46.
25. *Ibid.*, p. 47.
26. *Ibid.*
27. *Ibid.*, p. 332.
28. F.D. Maurice, *The Prayer Book and The Lord's Prayer* (Greenwood, S.C.: Attic Press, 1977).
29. See Paul Lehmann, *Ethics in a Christian Context* (New York: Harper & Row, 1963).
30. Maurice, *The Prayer Book*, p. xiii.
31. *Ibid.*, p. 4.
32. *Ibid.*, p. 5.
33. *Ibid.*, p. 7.
34. *Ibid.*, pp. 21, 22.
35. *Ibid.*, pp. 36, 37.
36. *Ibid.*, p. xv.
37. See *Vaclav Havel, Living in Truth: Twenty-Two Essays Published on the Occasion of the Award of the Erasmus Prize to Vaclav Havel.* Ed. Jan Vladislav (London: Faber & Faber, 1989).
38. See Søren Kierkegaard, *Training in Christianity* (Princeton: Princeton University Press, 1972).
39. Maurice, *The Prayer Book*, p. 10.
40. *Ibid.*, p. 12.
41. F.D. Maurice, *Theological Essays* (New York: Redfield, 1854), p. vii.
42. *Ibid.*, p. xvi.
43. *Ibid.*, pp. xviii, xix.
44. *Ibid.*, pp. xix, xx.
45. *Ibid.*, p. 3.
46. *Ibid.*, pp. 4, 5.
47. *Ibid.*, p. 7.
48. *Ibid.*
49. *Ibid.*, p. 10.
50. *Ibid.*, p. 11.
51. *Ibid.*, p. 13.
52. *Ibid.*, pp. 18-22.
53. *Ibid.*, p. 23.
54. *Ibid.*, p. 32.
55. *Ibid.*, p. 44.
56. *Ibid.*, p. 45.
57. *Ibid.*, p. 47.
58. *Ibid.*, p. 48.
59. *Ibid.*, p. 89.

60. *Ibid.*, p. 96.
61. *Ibid.*, pp. 124-139.
62. *Ibid.*, pp. 150, 151.
63. *Ibid.*, p. 162.
64. *Ibid.*, p. 173.
65. *Ibid.*, pp. 175-176.
66. *Ibid.*, pp. 177, 178.
67. *Ibid.*, pp. 182, 183.
68. *Ibid.*, p. 185.
69. *Ibid.*, p. 226.
70. *Ibid.*, p. 229.
71. *Ibid.*, p. 231.
72. *Ibid.*, pp. 235, 236.
73. *Ibid.*, p. 238.
74. *Ibid.*, p. 242.
75. *Ibid.*, p. 254.
76. *Ibid.*, p. 262.
77. *Ibid.*, p. 278.
78. *Ibid.*, p. 279.
79. *Ibid.*, p. 282.
80. *Ibid.*, p. 305.
81. *Ibid.*, p. 325.
82. *Ibid.*, p. 326.
83. *Ibid.*, p. 327.
84. *Ibid.*, p. 341.
85. *Ibid.*, pp. 342, 343.
86. *Ibid.*, p. 343.
87. *Ibid.*, p. 346.
88. F.D. Maurice, *The Kingdom of Christ* (London: James Clarke, 1959), Vol. 1, p. 245.
89. F.D. Maurice, *Moral and Metaphysical Philosophy* (London: Macmillan, 1882).
90. F.D. Maurice, *The Conscience* (London: Macmillan, 1872) and *Social Morality* (London: Macmillan, 1886).
91. Maurice, *The Conscience*, p. 1.
92. *Ibid.*, p. 2.
93. *Ibid.*, pp. 5, 6.
94. *Ibid.*, p. 14.
95. *Ibid.*, p. 26.
96. *Ibid.*, p. 47.
97. *Ibid.*, p. 94.
98. *Ibid.*, p. 99.
99. *Ibid.*, pp. 79, 80.
100. *Ibid.*, p. 174.
101. *Ibid.*, p. 175.
102. Maurice, *Social Morality*, p. xii.

103. Søren Kierkegaard, *Concluding Unscientific Postscript* (Princeton: Princeton University Press, 1971).

Chapter 4

1. F.D. Maurice, *Learning and Working* (London: Oxford University Press, 1968), p. 42.
2. *Ibid.*, p. 78.
3. *Ibid.*, p. 87.
4. *Ibid.*, p. 93.
5. *Ibid.*
6. *Ibid.*, p. 94.
7. *Ibid.*, p. 95.
8. *Ibid.*, p. 101.
9. *Ibid.*, p. 139.
10. *Ibid.*, p. 155.
11. G.D.H. Cole, *Socialist Thought: The Forerunners, 1789-1850; A History of Socialist Thought* (London: Macmillan, 1955) Vol. 1, p. 291.
12. Edward Norman, *The Victorian Christian Socialists* (Cambridge, England: Cambridge University Press, 1987), p. 14.

BIBLIOGRAPHY

Allen, P.R. "F.D. Maurice and J. M. Ludlow: A Reassessment of the Leaders of Christian Socialism," *Victorian Studies*, 11: 4 (June 1968), pp. 461-482.

Backstrom, Philip N. "The Practical Side of Christian Socialism in Victorian England," *Victorian Studies*, 6: 4 (June 1963), pp. 305-324.

Bax, E. Belfort. *Ethics of Socialism, being Further Essays in Modern Socialist Criticism, &c.* 2nd ed. London: Swan Sonnenschein & Co., 1891.

Beer, Max. *A History of British Socialism.* 2 vols. New York: Arno Press, 1979 [1920]. Reprint of the 1930 edition published by G. Bell, London. Based on *Geschichte des sozialismus in England* (1912).

Bernstein, Eduard. *Cromwell and Communism: Socialism and Democracy in the Great English Revolution.* Translated by H.J. Stenning. London: George Allen & Unwin, Ltd., 1930. Translation of the 4th ed. of *Sozialismus und Demokratie in der grossen englischen Revolution* (1922).

Bevan, Ruth A. *Marx and Burke: A Revisionist View.* LaSalle, Ill.: Open Court, 1973.

Booth, Harry Fehr. *The Knowledge of God and the Practice of Society in F.D. Maurice.* Ph.D. Dissertation, Boston University, 1963.

Boulger, James D. *Coleridge as Religious Thinker.* New Haven, Conn.: Yale University Press, 1961.

Briggs, Asa. *Victorian Cities.* New York: Harper, 1970. (1st ed. 1963).

_____. *Victorian People: A Reassessment of Persons and Themes, 1851-1867.* Rev. ed. Chicago: University of Chicago Press, 1970. (1st ed. 1955).

Brookfield, Frances M. *The Cambridge "Apostles."* London: Sir Isaac Pitman & Sons, Ltd., 1906.

Brose, Olive. "F.D. Maurice and the Victorian Crisis of Belief," *Victorian Studies*, 3: 3 (March 1960), pp. 227-248.

_____. *F.D. Maurice: Rebellious Conformist, 1805-1872.* Athens, Ohio: Ohio University Press, 1971.

Carlyle, Thomas. *Past and Present.* Ed. Richard D. Altick. New York: New York University Press, 1965 [1843].

BIBLIOGRAPHY

The Challenge of Socialism. 2nd ed. Edited by Henry Pelling. London: Adam & Charles Black, 1964.

Christensen, Torben. *The Divine Order: A Study in F.D. Maurice's Theology.* Leiden: E.J. Brill, 1973.

_____. *Origin and History of Christian Socialism, 1848-1854.* Aarhus: Universitaetsforlaget, 1962.

Cole, G.D.H. *Socialist Thought: The Forerunners, 1789-1850.* A History of Socialist Thought, Vol. 1. London: Macmillan, 1955.

Coleridge, Samuel Taylor. *Aids to Reflection. The Collected Works of Samuel Taylor Coleridge,* Vol. 9. Ed. John Beer. Princeton, N.J.: Princeton University Press, 1993 [1825].

_____. *Biographia Literaria, or, biographical sketches of my literary life and opinions. The Collected Works of Samuel Taylor Coleridge,* Vol. 7. Ed. James Engell and W. Jackson Bate. Princeton, N.J.: Princeton University Press, 1983 [1817].

_____. *Lay Sermons. The Collected Works of Samuel Taylor Coleridge,* Vol. 6. Ed. R.J. White. Princeton, N.J.: Princeton University Press, 1972. Includes *The Statesman's Manual* (1816) and *A Lay Sermon* (1817).

_____. *On the Constitution of the Church and State.* 2nd ed. *The Collected Works of Samuel Taylor Coleridge,* Vol. 10. Ed. John Colmer. Princeton, N.J.: Princeton University Press, 1976 [1830]. (1st ed. 1829).

Courtney, Janet E. *Freethinkers of the Nineteenth Century.* New York: E.P. Dutton, 1920.

Crouzet, François. *The Victorian Economy.* Translated by A.S. Forster. New York: Columbia University Press, 1982. Translation of *L'Economie de la Grande-Bretagne victorienne.*

Dorrien, Gary J. *The Democratic Socialist Vision.* Totowa, N.J.: Rowman & Littlefield, 1986.

_____. *Reconstructing the Common Good: Theology and the Social Order.* Maryknoll, N.Y.: Orbis Books, 1990.

_____. *Soul in Society: The Making and Renewal of Social Christianity.* Minneapolis, Minn.: Fortress Press, 1995.

Fabian Essays in Socialism. Ed. Bernard Shaw. London: George Allen & Unwin Ltd., 1948 [1889].

Finn, Margot C. *After Chartism: Class and Nation in English Radical Politics, 1848-1874*. Cambridge, England: Cambridge University Press, 1993.

Grylls, Rosalie Glynn. *Queen's College, 1848-1948*. London: George Routledge & Sons, Ltd., 1948.

Hall, Robert Tom. *The Unity of Philosophy, Theology, and Ethics in the Thought of Frederick Denison Maurice*. Ph.D. Dissertation, Drew University, 1967.

Harrington, Michael. *Socialism: Past and Future*. New York: Plume, 1989.

Harrison, J.F.C. *A History of the Working Men's College, 1854-1954*. London: Routledge & Kegan Paul, 1954.

Himmelfarb, Gertrude. *The Idea of Poverty: England in the Early Industrial Age*. New York: Alfred A. Knopf, 1983.

_____. *Marriage & Morals among the Victorians*. New York: Alfred A. Knopf, 1986.

_____. *Poverty and Compassion: The Moral Imagination of the Late Victorians*. New York: Alfred A. Knopf, 1991.

Houghton, Walter E. *The Victorian Frame of Mind, 1830-1870*. New Haven, Conn.: Yale University Press, 1957.

Ketchum, Robert. *F.D. Maurice: An Assessment of His Contributions to Nineteenth-Century English Education*. Ph.D. Dissertation, Syracuse University, 1969.

The Life of Frederick Denison Maurice, Chiefly Told in His Own Letters. 2 vol. Ed. Frederick Maurice. London: Macmillan, 1884.

McClain, Frank Mauldin. *Maurice: Man and Moralist*. London: SPCK, 1972.

McIntyre, Mary Louise. *Theology and Politics in F.D. Maurice's Early Thought, 1825-1846*. Ph.D. Dissertation, Northwestern University, 1995.

Marx, Karl and Frederick Engels. *Selected Works*. New York: International Publishers, 1968. [Includes *Manifesto of the Communist Party* (1848) and *Socialism: Utopian and Scientific* (1877-1878, 1st English ed. 1892).]

Mathias, Peter. *The First Industrial Nation: An Economic History of Britain, 1700-1914*. 2nd ed. London: Methuen, 1983.

Maurice, Frederick Denison. *The Conscience: Lectures on Casuistry, Delivered in the University of Cambridge*. 2nd ed. London: Macmillan, 1872.

_____. *The Kingdom of Christ*. 2 vols. 2nd ed. London: James Clarke & Co., Ltd., 1959 [1842]. (1st ed. 1838).

_____. *Learning and Working*. London: Oxford University Press, 1968 [1855].

_____. *Moral and Metaphysical Philosophy*. 2 vols. London: Macmillan, 1882 [1862].

_____. *The Prayer Book and The Lord's Prayer*. Greenwood, S.C.: Attic Press, 1977. (The sermons on the Prayer Book were originally delivered in 1848).

_____. *Social Morality: Twenty-One Lectures Delivered in the University of Cambridge*. London: Macmillan, 1869.

_____. *Theological Essays*. New York: Redfield, 1854. [From the 2nd London ed. (Macmillan, 1853)].

Mill, John Stuart. *Autobiography*. London: Longmans, Green, Reader, and Dyer, 1873.

_____. *On Bentham & Coleridge*. New York: Harper, 1962. Reprint of *Mill On Bentham and Coleridge*, published by Chatto & Windus, London, 1950. The essays are taken from Mill's *Dissertations and Discussions* (1865).

Morrow, John. *Coleridge's Political Thought: Property, Morality, and the Limits of Traditional Discourse*. New York: St. Martin's Press, 1990.

Muirhead, John H. *Coleridge as Philosopher*. New York: Macmillan, 1930.

Norman, E.R. *Church and Society in England, 1770-1970: A Historical Study*. London: Oxford University Press, 1976.

Norman, Edward. *The Victorian Christian Socialists*. Cambridge, England: Cambridge University Press, 1987.

Perkins, Mary Ann. *Coleridge's Philosophy: The Logos as Unifying Principle*. London: Oxford University Press, 1994.

Stanley Pierson. *British Socialists: The Journey from Fantasy to Politics*. Cambridge, Mass.: Harvard University Press, 1979.

_____. *Marxism and the Origins of British Socialism: The Struggle for a New Consciousness*. Ithaca, N.Y.: Cornell University Press, 1973.

Pugh, Ralph A. *The Constitutive Principles of Early Victorian Christian Socialism, 1848-1854*. 2 vols. Ph.D. Dissertation, University of Chicago, 1994.

Bibliography 97

Ramsey, Arthur Michael. *F.D. Maurice and the Conflicts of Modern Theology.* Cambridge, England: Cambridge University Press, 1951.

Raven, Charles E. *Christian Socialism, 1848-1854.* New York: Augustus M. Kelley, 1968 [1920].

Reckitt, Maurice B. *Maurice to Temple: A Century of the Social Movement in the Church of England.* Scott Holland Memorial Lectures, 1946. London: Faber and Faber, Ltd., 1946.

"Revolutionary Literature," *Quarterly Review*, 89: 178 (September 1851), pp. 491-543.

Rostow, W.W. *The Stages of Economic Growth: A Non-Communist Manifesto.* 3rd ed. Cambridge, England: Cambridge University Press, 1990. (1st ed. 1960.)

Sanders, Charles Richard. *Coleridge and the Broad Church Movement.* Durham, N.C.: Duke University Press, 1942.

Sangster, Paul. *A History of the Free Churches.* London: Heinemann, 1983.

Simmons, David D. *Politics for the People as Rhetorical Response by the Victorian Christian Socialists to the Chartist Movement.* Ph.D. Dissertation. Florida State University, 1996.

Sokolof, Nancy. *Revelation as Education in the Thought of F.D. Maurice.* Ph.D. Dissertation, Columbia University, 1971.

Swanston, Hamish F.G. *Ideas of Order: Anglicans and the Renewal of Theological Method in the Middle Years of the Nineteenth Century.* Assen, The Netherlands: Van Gorcum & Co., B.V., 1974.

Thomas, Roger. "The Non-Subscription Controversy Amongst Dissenters in 1719: The Salters' Hall Debate," *Journal of Ecclesiastical History*, 4: 2 (October 1953), pp. 162-186.

Thompson, Dorothy. *The Chartists: Popular Politics in the Industrial Revolution.* New York: Pantheon, 1984.

Toynbee, Arnold. *Lectures on the Industrial Revolution of the Eighteenth Century in England: Popular Addresses, Notes, and Other Fragments.* London: Longmans, Green, and Co., 1906.

Ulam, Adam B. *Philosophical Foundations of English Socialism.* New York: Octagon Books, 1964.

Walvin, James. *Victorian Values.* London: Sphere Books Ltd., 1988.

Wedgewood, Julia. *Nineteenth-Century Teachers and Other Essays*. London: Hodder and Stoughton, 1909.

Wiener, Martin J. *English Culture and the Decline of the Industrial Spirit, 1850-1980*. Cambridge, England: Cambridge University Press, 1981.

Wolf, William J. *The Spirit of Anglicanism: Hooker, Maurice, Temple*. Wilton, Conn.: Morehouse-Barlow, 1979.

Wordsworth, William. *Lyrical Ballads, 1798*. Ed. W. J. B. Owen. 2nd ed. London: Oxford University Press, 1969.

Young, David. *F.D. Maurice and Unitarianism*. London: Oxford University Press, 1992.

ABOUT THE AUTHOR

Steven Schroeder is Associate Professor of Religion and Philosophy at Capital University in Ohio. He is the author of two previous books (*A Community and a Perspective: Lutheran Peace Fellowship and the Edge of the Church, 1941-1991* and *Virginia Woolf's Subject and the Subject of Ethics*), as well as numerous scholarly articles in philosophy and religious studies. His poetry has appeared in *Georgetown Review, Halcyon, Mosaic, Rambunctious Review,* and the *Emily Dickinson Award Anthology*.

INDEX

Abraham, 52, 54
absolute monarchy, 11, 20
accumulation, 19, 73, 77
Act of Uniformity
    of 1549, 4
    of 1662, 7
adult baptism, 6
adult education, 18, 73, 74, 76, 77
agricultural economy, 21
Aids to Reflection, 42-45, 47
Alexander of Hales, 24
Alfred (King of England), 74
alienation, 49, 60, 61
American Revolution, 17
Ames, William, 6
Anglican, Anglicanism, 4-6, 9, 14, 20, 26, 44, 61, 82
Anne (Queen of England), 9
antithesis, 44, 45
Aquinas, Thomas, 24
Aristotle, 29, 33
Arkwright, Richard, 77
Arminian, Arminianism, 6, 7, 9
Arminius, Jacobus, 6
Arnold, Matthew, 26
associationism, 30
atonement, 62, 65
Augustinian, 22, 38
autobiography, 14, 29
axiological turn, 23

Bacon, Francis, 11, 14
Balliol College (Oxford), 3
baptism, 6, 9, 49, 54-57
Baptist, 4, 6, 9, 54
Becket, Thomas, 3
Beer, Max, 24, 26
Benbow, William, 13
Benedictine Rule, 76
Bentham, Jeremy, 23, 24
Berkeley, George, 31, 36
biblicism, 5, 51

Biographia Literaria, 29, 30, 36, 40, 42-47
Boethius, 75
Böhme, Jakob, 37
Bolshevik Revolution, 16
Book of Common Prayer, 4, 58
Book of Discipline, 5
bourgeoisie, 11, 12, 17, 18, 20
Bradshaw, William, 6
Briggs, Asa, 21
Britain, 7, 17, 18, 21, 22, 47, 74, 78, 83
Burke, Edmund, 17

Calvin, John, 6, 11, 50
Calvinism, 5, 8, 9, 11, 12, 14, 17, 20
Calvinist, 2-7, 9, 14, 20, 51
Cambridge, 1, 9, 15, 24, 38, 44, 70, 78
Cambridge Platonism, 15, 44
capital, 77
capitalism, 11, 12, 17-20, 22, 24, 82, 83
Carlyle, Thomas, 20, 26
Catholic, 3, 5, 14, 49, 50
Catholicism, 4, 7, 9, 17
centralization, 18
ceremony, 3, 4, 6
Charlemagne, 74
Charles I, 6
Charles II, 7
Chartism, 12, 13
Christensen, Torben, 82
Christian Socialism, 10-14, 18, 20, 58, 70, 81, 82
Christian Socialist, 13, 18, 25, 61, 73
Christianity, 8, 20, 50-52, 56, 69, 72
Church, 1-11, 14, 20, 47, 49, 50, 52-54, 58-64, 66-68, 80, 82
Church of England, 1, 4, 8, 10, 58, 61
citizen, 64, 77
civil society, 23
civilization, 69, 73, 74, 79
Clark, Samuel, 49

INDEX

clerisy, 54, 74
Cole, G.D.H., 81
Coleridge, Samuel Taylor, 9, 10, 15, 17, 20, 23-27, 29-40, 42-47, 49, 50, 52, 54, 61, 62, 74, 76, 79, 82
colleges, 1, 75
commodification, 18
commodities, 19, 20
communal, 25, 26, 51, 53, 70, 72
communication, 38, 41, 46, 78
communion, 9, 50, 58
communism, 12
community, 13, 64, 70, 75, 79, 80
competition, 20, 60
composition, 41, 45
comprehension, 34, 36, 41, 45, 46, 57, 63
compromise, 58-61
Congregational, 4, 6, 7
Conscience, 70-72
conservative, 10, 12, 14, 80, 81
constitution, 25, 47-50, 52-54, 65
Constitution of Church and State, 47, 50
consumption, 19
containment, 32, 51, 82, 83
continuity, 35
cooperation, 20, 48
cooperatives, 10
corruption, 24, 25
covenant, 52, 53, 55-58
creed, 2, 5, 8, 11, 14, 20, 58, 63, 67
critical theory, 29, 30, 39
Cromwell, Oliver, 6, 7

Darwin, Charles, 12
democracy, 17, 18, 37, 54
derivative sovereignty, 23
Descartes, René, 32, 33, 35, 37
description, 9, 12, 17, 26, 31, 32, 37, 55, 56, 79
digger, 26, 46
digging, 26, 37, 40, 42, 81, 83
direct action, 26
disciple, 24, 55
disciple at second hand, 55
disciplined activity, 76

disposition, 32, 33
distinction, 15, 17, 24, 31, 35, 36, 38, 40, 41, 43-45, 52, 53, 59, 61, 62, 68, 70
doctrine, 3, 4, 6, 8, 58, 61
dogmatism, 37
Dominican, 24
Dublin, 9
Dühring, Eugen, 11
Duns Scotus, 11, 24
dynamic philosophy, 29, 31

ecological psychology, 30
economics, 16
ecumenical, 9
education, 5, 10, 14, 18, 38, 48, 54, 73-80
education for adulthood, 75, 79
education of children, 74, 75
Edward VI, 4
eighteenth century, 2, 17, 23
election, 50, 51
electoral politics, 47
Elizabeth (Queen of England), 4, 5
Elizabethan settlement, 4
empiricist, 12, 15
Engels, Frederick, 11-16, 20, 25
English socialism, 11, 12
episcopacy, 5, 6
episcopal polity, 3
Episcopalian, 1
epistemological, 31, 39, 82
Erskine, Thomas, 9
essential poetry, 40
eternal punishment, 68, 81
eternity, 68
ethical, 23, 26, 27, 34, 37-39, 58, 61, 72, 82
ethics, 39, 58, 60, 61, 72, 79-82
Ethics in a Christian Context, 58
Eucharist, 54-57
Europe, 3, 12, 20, 51, 83
Eustace Conway, 9
Evangelical, 9, 10
exchange, 19, 72
exchange value, 19
exclusive, 31, 59, 61, 63-65

expedience, 43
experience, 8, 15, 22, 31, 40, 50, 62, 76
experimental psychology, 32
external, 31-33, 36

Fabianism, 12, 14
Fabians, 13, 17, 19
factory reform, 18
factory system, 18, 21, 22
faith, 12, 13, 19, 44-46, 49, 51, 52, 62, 65, 76, 81
Fall, the, 24, 25, 49, 59, 60
family, 8, 9, 44, 52, 53, 64
family relationships, 53
fancy, 37, 39, 40, 71
feudalism, 11, 17, 18, 25
Feuerbach, Ludwig, 37
Fox, George, 37, 51
France, 1, 4, 5, 7, 11, 73
Francis II, 5
Franciscan, 24
freedom, 6, 7, 14, 20, 25, 37-39, 42, 43, 46, 47, 52, 57, 68, 69, 75, 78, 79, 82
freedom of worship, 7
French Revolution, 11, 12, 15-17, 21, 23, 26
French socialism, 81

Gassendi, Pierre, 31
Geneva, 5
geography, 79
Germany, 2, 11
Glorious Revolution, 17, 22
Goethe, Johann Wolfgang von, 30
government, 3, 6, 66, 68, 80
grace, 24, 25
grammar schools, 75, 76
gravity, 32, 35, 41
Great Britain, 7, 21, 22

habit, 33, 43, 63, 68, 78
Hampton Court, 5
Hare, Julius, 15
harmony, 34, 35, 41
Harrington, Michael, 22

Hartley, David, 11, 32, 33, 36
head, 3, 10, 43, 64, 82
heart, 9, 10, 24, 30, 38, 43
Hegel, G.F.W., 31, 37, 44, 45
Hegelian, 15, 31
hell, 25, 65
Helwys, Thomas, 6
Henry VIII, 3, 4, 6
higher education for women, 10
historical development, 11, 12, 16
history, 1-3, 5, 7, 9-12, 21, 24, 36, 47, 50, 52-54, 56-58, 67, 71, 79-81
History of British Socialism, 24
Hobbes, Thomas, 11, 31-33, 37
Holland, 4, 6
home, 9, 58, 61, 75
Hooker, Richard, 5
human choice, 6
human nature, 12, 31
human will, 23, 53
humanity, 13, 25, 49-54, 66, 71
Hume, David, 32, 33, 37
hylozoism, 35

"I", 70, 71
idea, 20, 32, 36, 45, 50, 51, 55, 57, 66, 71
idealism, 30, 31, 37, 39
idealist, 36
identity, 3, 39, 45, 54
imagination, 34-36, 39, 40, 42, 45, 46
incarnation, 12, 20, 50, 51, 53, 56, 57, 59, 69, 72
inclusive, 59, 61, 63
Independents, 2
indifference, 45
individual, 2, 15, 16, 19, 22, 23, 26, 50-52, 64, 70-72
individualism, 15, 22
industrial economy, 21
Industrial Revolution, 16, 19, 23
infant baptism, 6
infant education, 75, 76
intelligence, 39
intelligentsia, 83, 85, 86
internal, 31, 33, 36
internal relations, 31

invisible hand, 23
inward light, 50, 51
Ireland, 7
isolation, 64

Jacob, Henry, 6
James I (James VI of Scotland), 5
James II, 7
journalism, 1, 9, 46, 82
justification, 50, 51

Kant, Immanuel, 37, 38, 44, 45
Kantian, 15, 37
Kepler, Johannes, 32
Kierkegaard, Søren, 72
Kingdom of Christ, 15, 21, 49, 55, 57, 58, 62, 72
King's College, 25, 62, 73, 80, 82
Knox, John, 4, 5

labor, 19, 23, 25, 31, 76, 77, 81
labor theory of value, 23
laissez-faire, 14, 19, 20, 25
language, 1, 3, 9, 32, 38-42, 46, 57, 63-65, 75, 80
Laud, William, 6
Law, William, 37
law of association, 32, 33, 35, 40
Learning and Working, 76-78
Lehmann, Paul, 58
Leibniz, Gottfried, 35, 36
Leighton, Robert, 44, 45
leisure, 74, 76, 77
Lenin, Vladimir, 16
liturgy, 4, 6, 59-61
locality, 53, 75
Locke, John, 8, 11, 12, 14, 15, 22, 24, 25, 36, 45
Lockean empiricism, 15, 16
London, 1, 13, 14, 18, 22, 43, 58, 73
London Debating Society, 14, 43
London Working Men's Association, 13
Louis Bonaparte, 13
Ludlow, John, 26, 73, 81
Luther, Martin, 11, 20, 25, 38, 50, 51, 68

Lutheran, 3, 11, 14, 21, 51
Lutheran Reformation, 11
Lutheranism, 14, 20
Lyrical Ballads, 30, 42

machine, 17, 76, 77
Mackintosh, James, 32
Magna Carta, 17
Manicheism, 66
Mao Tse-Tung, 16
Martineau, James, 10, 50
Marx, Karl, 11-15, 20, 25, 31, 37, 44
Marxist socialism, 12
Marxist theory, 17, 19
Mary I (Queen of England), 4, 5
Mary II (Queen of England), 7, 23
Mary (Queen of Scots), 5
materialism, 11, 14, 30, 31, 35-37, 39
mathematics, 45, 77, 79, 80
matter, 2, 3, 15, 20, 32, 35, 36, 38, 40, 44, 46, 52, 54, 56, 61, 65, 70, 72, 77, 80
Maurice, Frederick, 1, 2, 6-9, 11, 14, 16
Maurice, Michael, 1, 2, 4, 7, 8, 10
Maurice, Priscilla, 8, 9
means of production, 19, 20
mechanistic, 32, 44, 47, 48
memory, 32-34, 40, 79
mendicant orders, 75
mesothesis, 44, 45
metaphysical, 26, 27, 32, 48, 69, 81, 82
method, 15, 44, 45, 52, 60, 62, 65, 72, 79
middle class, 13, 18
Mill, John Stuart, 12, 14, 15, 19, 20, 26, 43, 82
mind, 2, 3, 8, 21, 29-32, 35, 40, 56, 59, 60, 68, 78, 80
miscellaneous man, 73, 77
monarchy, 7, 11, 20, 23, 25, 47
monasticism, 24, 76
money, 19, 79
Moral and Metaphysical Philosophy, 69
moral development, 38

Index

moral education, 38
moral goodness, 43
moral stages, 24
Moravian, 9
More, Henry, 44
motivation, 19
Müntzer, Thomas, 11
Murton, John, 6
mysticism, 37

national church, 3, 50
national sovereignty, 4
nationalism, 30
necessity, 12, 39, 46, 57, 65, 66
New Testament, 3
Newport Rising, 13
Newton, Isaac, 8, 32
nineteenth century, 10, 16, 17, 21-23, 25, 26, 31, 56, 61
Nonconformity, 7

objects, 32, 33, 36, 37, 40, 43, 44, 46, 64, 73, 79
Ockham, William, 24, 25
ontological, 31, 39
opposition, 6, 7, 11, 20, 26, 31, 45, 50, 77
optics, 36
order, 3, 14, 24, 30, 35, 38, 39, 43, 45, 61, 70-72, 75, 77, 79, 80, 82
ordination, 1, 10, 82
organic, 17, 27, 47
organic commonwealth, 27
organism, 17
organs of sense, 37, 38
organs of spirit, 38
orthodoxy, 9, 14, 30, 44, 58, 62
Owen, Robert, 22, 26
Oxford, 3, 9, 15, 24, 49
Oxford Movement, 49

Paine, Thomas, 17, 47
Paradise, 24
Parliament, 5-7, 13, 17
Parliamentary Reform Act (1832), 10, 12
party, 3-5, 10, 49, 58, 65

peasantry, 25, 26
peasants, 11
pedagogy, 58
perceptual mechanisms, 36
perceptual theory, 30, 31
periodization, 21
person, 10, 35, 38, 50, 52, 55-57, 60, 63-66, 68, 70-73, 76, 78, 80
personality, 51
philosophic consciousness, 37, 42
philosophy, 11, 22-25, 29-32, 36, 37, 39-41, 44-48, 69-72, 80
philosophy of history, 24
philosophy of time, 25
Pierson, Stanley, 26
Plato, 15, 33
Platonic ideal, 24
Platonist, 15
play, 76
pleasure, 40, 41
poetic genius, 40
poetry, 30, 39-42, 46, 47, 80
Political Economy, 14, 23, 43, 49
politics, 5, 10, 16, 18, 26, 30, 42, 47, 71, 74, 79
polity, 1-5, 7, 14, 42, 51
popular sovereignty, 23, 25, 26
population, 18, 21
position, 6, 11, 24, 25, 43, 45, 53, 55, 66, 71, 80, 82
practical wisdom, 75
prayer, 4, 56, 58, 59, 61
preaching orders, 24
Presbyterian, 1, 2, 4-6, 8
presence, 25, 31, 35, 53, 55, 57, 58
Price, Richard, 10, 17
priesthood, 53
Priestley, Joseph, 2, 10, 11, 14, 33
primary imagination, 39, 40
principle, 14, 23, 43, 50-52, 56, 59, 61, 67, 69, 72, 80
production, 18-22, 45
property, 22-25, 71
prophetic tradition, 54
prose, 41
Protestant Reformation, 2, 3, 11, 16
prothesis, 45

prudence, 43
public, 18, 20, 22, 29, 30, 52, 55, 63, 70, 74, 80
public ownership, 20
public sovereignty, 22
Pugh, Ralph, 81
Puritan, 5, 6
pursuit of happiness, 23
Pusey, William, 49
Pythagorean, 44

Quaker, 9, 49-51
Queen's College, 18

railroad, 21
rationalist, 17, 37
realism, 25, 39
reason, 6-9, 13, 17, 20, 23-26, 33, 37, 39, 41, 43-46, 62, 67
reasonableness, 5
Reformation, 2-4, 11, 16, 20, 24, 25, 50, 51, 55, 76, 79
religion, 8, 16, 26, 43, 45, 63
representation, 13, 17, 18, 21, 32, 33, 37
revivalism, 10
revolution, 1, 11-13, 15-17, 19, 21-23, 26
Romantic, 9, 26, 30
Romanticism, 10, 20, 26
Rome, 3, 4, 75
rural, 18, 21
Ruskin, John, 26
Russia, 16

sacrifice, 5, 56, 57, 66
saints, 7, 25, 58
Saul of Tarsus, 65
Saxon education, 74
Schlegel, Friedrich von, 10
Scholastic theology, 26
science, 12, 39, 41, 43, 71, 72, 78
science of words, 43
Scotland, 2-7
Scottish General Assembly, 5, 6
Scripture, 3-8, 50, 52, 53, 67
secondary imagination, 39

sectarianism, 38, 60
self, 13, 19-21, 29, 38, 39, 50, 53, 60, 66, 77
self-interest, 19
Separatist, 5, 6, 58
Shelley, Mary, 26
sin, 25, 62, 64, 65, 68
sixteenth century, 2, 3, 75
skepticism, 37
slavery, 71
Smith, Adam, 12
Social Morality, 70-72
socialism, 10-15, 18-20, 24, 26, 30, 31, 48, 58, 70, 73, 81-83
Socialism: Utopian and Scientific, 11, 13
socialization, 22
society, 9, 14, 15, 18, 20-23, 26, 43, 48-55, 58, 62, 64-66, 68, 70-72, 78, 79
Society of Friends, 49, 58
Socinian, 6, 8
Socinus, Faustus (Sozzini), 6, 8
solitude, 64
soul, 34, 35, 38, 40, 42, 43, 45, 46, 67, 77
Southwark, 6
sovereign, 3, 4, 7, 14
sovereignty of God, 2
Sozzini (Socinus), 6
Spirit, 15, 24, 30, 38, 39, 43, 53, 55, 58, 67-69, 76
spiritual constitution, 52-54
spontaneous consciousness, 37, 40
Stalin, Joseph, 20
State, 3, 12, 14, 17, 20, 23, 25, 34, 47, 50, 52, 64, 65, 68, 72
Statesman's Manual, 47
Stoic, 24
suffrage, 10, 13
Supremacy Act (1534), 3
survival, 19
synthesis, 45
system, 6, 15, 17-19, 21, 22, 27, 34-36, 49, 51, 52, 57, 58, 60, 62, 66, 72, 78, 82

Taylor, Harriet, 14
teachers, 70, 76, 79, 80
teaching, 1, 25, 55, 64, 76
Tennyson, Alfred, 61
Thatcher, Margaret, 10
Theological Essays, 25, 61, 73, 81
theology, 3-5, 11, 24, 26, 30, 58, 61-63, 68, 69, 72, 80, 81
theory, 17, 19, 23, 29-32, 38, 39, 42, 47, 51, 54, 58, 73, 80-82
thesis, 44, 45
Thirty-Nine Articles, 4, 6, 7, 9, 59
time, 25, 32, 33, 35, 68, 72, 80, 81
Toleration Act, 7
Tories, 14
Tractarians, 26
transcendental philosophy, 30, 31, 37, 39
transubstantiation, 7
triadic structure, 44
trinity, 2, 6, 8
turning the soul, 38

understanding, 34, 39, 43-46, 62
Unitarian, 1, 2, 4, 8-10, 31, 50, 51, 58
United States, 17, 18, 71
universal, 15, 49-58, 61, 65
universal society, 51-55, 65
universities, 24, 75, 76, 80
University of Berlin, 11
University of London, 1
urban, 18, 20, 21
urbanization, 21, 22
Utilitarians, 14, 15
utility, 79

value, 15, 19, 23, 43
Victorian, 1, 10-12, 16, 18, 19, 21, 22, 32
violent revolution, 26
vision, 33, 36
vocation, 78

wages, 19
wealth, 19, 78
Webb, Sydney, 13
Welfare State, 12, 20

Wesley, John, 8
Westminster Assembly, 6
Westminster Confession, 2, 6
William and Mary, 7, 23
William of Orange, 7
women's suffrage, 10
Wordsworth, William, 9, 30, 40, 42, 61
work, 19, 23, 61-64, 69, 74-79, 85, 86
working class, 13, 18, 73, 78
Working Men's College, 10, 18, 73, 74, 78, 81
worship, 2, 4, 7, 58, 59, 61, 66, 77
writing, 1, 9, 22, 29, 30, 38, 41, 46, 47, 62, 76
written language, 9
Wycliffe, John, 3, 24, 25, 75

Zwingli, Ulrich, 50
Zwinglian, 3, 4

VIBS

The **Value Inquiry Book Series** is co-sponsored by:

American Maritain Association
American Society for Value Inquiry
Association for Personalist Studies
Association for Process Philosophy of Education
Center for East European Dialogue and Development, Rochester Institute of Technology
Centre for Cultural Research, Aarhus University
College of Education and Allied Professions, Bowling Green State University
Concerned Philosophers for Peace
Conference of Philosophical Societies
Institute of Philosophy of the High Council of Scientific Research, Spain
International Academy of Philosophy of the Principality of Liechtenstein
International Society for Universalism
Natural Law Society
Philosophical Society of Finland
Philosophy Born of Struggle Association
Philosophy Seminar, University of Mainz
R.S. Hartman Institute for Formal and Applied Axiology
Society for Iberian and Latin-American Thought
Society for the Philosophic Study of Genocide and the Holocaust
Society for the Philosophy of Sex and Love
Yves R. Simon Institute.

Titles Published

1. Noel Balzer, *The Human Being as a Logical Thinker.*

2. Archie J. Bahm, *Axiology: The Science of Values.*

3. H. P. P. (Hennie) Lötter, *Justice for an Unjust Society.*

4. H. G. Callaway, *Context for Meaning and Analysis: A Critical Study in the Philosophy of Language.*

5. Benjamin S. Llamzon, *A Humane Case for Moral Intuition.*

6. James R. Watson, *Between Auschwitz and Tradition: Postmodern Reflections on the Task of Thinking.* A volume in **Holocaust and Genocide Studies.**

7. Robert S. Hartman, *Freedom to Live: The Robert Hartman Story,* edited by Arthur R. Ellis. A volume in **Hartman Institute Axiology Studies.**

8. Archie J. Bahm, *Ethics: The Science of Oughtness.*

9. George David Miller, *An Idiosyncratic Ethics; Or, the Lauramachean Ethics.*

10. Joseph P. DeMarco, *A Coherence Theory in Ethics.*

11. Frank G. Forrest, *Valuemetrics$^{\aleph}$: The Science of Personal and Professional Ethics.* A volume in **Hartman Institute Axiology Studies.**

12. William Gerber, *The Meaning of Life: Insights of the World's Great Thinkers.*

13. Richard T. Hull, Editor, *A Quarter Century of Value Inquiry: Presidential Addresses of the American Society for Value Inquiry.* A volume in **Histories and Addresses of Philosophical Societies.**

14. William Gerber, *Nuggets of Wisdom from Great Jewish Thinkers: From Biblical Times to the Present.*

15. Sidney Axinn, *The Logic of Hope: Extensions of Kant's View of Religion.*

16. Messay Kebede, *Meaning and Development.*

17. Amihud Gilead, *The Platonic Odyssey: A Philosophical-Literary Inquiry into the Phaedo.*

18. Necip Fikri Alican, *Mill's Principle of Utility: A Defense of John Stuart Mill's Notorious Proof.* A volume in **Universal Justice.**

19. Michael H. Mitias, Editor, *Philosophy and Architecture.*

20. Roger T. Simonds, *Rational Individualism: The Perennial Philosophy of Legal Interpretation.* A volume in **Natural Law Studies.**

21. William Pencak, *The Conflict of Law and Justice in the Icelandic Sagas.*

22. Samuel M. Natale and Brian M. Rothschild, Editors, *Values, Work, Education: The Meanings of Work.*

23. N. Georgopoulos and Michael Heim, Editors, *Being Human in the Ultimate: Studies in the Thought of John M. Anderson.*

24. Robert Wesson and Patricia A. Williams, Editors, *Evolution and Human Values.*

25. Wim J. van der Steen, *Facts, Values, and Methodology: A New Approach to Ethics.*

26. Avi Sagi and Daniel Statman, *Religion and Morality.*

27. Albert William Levi, *The High Road of Humanity: The Seven Ethical Ages of Western Man*, edited by Donald Phillip Verene and Molly Black Verene.

28. Samuel M. Natale and Brian M. Rothschild, Editors, *Work Values: Education, Organization, and Religious Concerns.*

29. Laurence F. Bove and Laura Duhan Kaplan, Editors, *From the Eye of the Storm: Regional Conflicts and the Philosophy of Peace.* A volume in **Philosophy of Peace.**

30. Robin Attfield, *Value, Obligation, and Meta-Ethics.*

31. William Gerber, *The Deepest Questions You Can Ask About God: As Answered by the World's Great Thinkers.*

Teachers and Students. Epilogue by Mark Roelof Eleveld. A volume in **Philosophy of Education.**

63. William Gerber, *Love, Poetry, and Immortality: Luminous Insights of the World's Great Thinkers.*

64. Dane R. Gordon, Editor, *Philosophy in Post-Communist Europe.* A volume in **Post-Communist European Thought.**

65. Dane R. Gordon and Józef Niżnik, Editors, Criticism and Defense of Rationality in Contemporary Philosophy. A volume in **Post-Communist European Thought.**

66. John R. Shook, *Pragmatism: An Annotated Bibliography, 1898-1940.* With Contributions by E. Paul Colella, Lesley Friedman, Frank X. Ryan, and Ignas K. Skrupskelis.

67. Lansana Keita, *The Human Project and the Temptations of Science.*

68. Michael M. Kazanjian, *Phenomenology and Education: Cosmology, Co-Being, and Core Curriculum.* A volume in **Philosophy of Education.**

69. James W. Vice, *The Reopening of the American Mind: On Skepticism and Constitutionalism.*

70. Sarah Bishop Merrill, *Defining Personhood: Toward the Ethics of Quality in Clinical Care.*

71. Dane R. Gordon, *Philosophy and Vision.*

72. Alan Milchman and Alan Rosenberg, Editors, *Postmodernism and the Holocaust.* A volume in **Holocaust and Genocide Studies.**

73. Peter A. Redpath, *Masquerade of the Dream Walkers: Prophetic Theology from the Cartesians to Hegel.* A volume in **Studies in the History of Western Philosophy.**

74. Malcolm D. Evans, *Whitehead and Philosophy of Education: The Seamless Coat of Learning.* A volume in **Philosophy of Education.**

75. Warren E. Steinkraus, *Taking Religious Claims Seriously: A Philosophy of Religion*, edited by Michael H. Mitias. A volume in **Universal Justice.**

76. Thomas Magnell, Editor, *Values and Education.*

77. Kenneth A. Bryson, *Persons and Immortality.* A volume in **Natural Law Studies**.

78. Steven V. Hicks, *International Law and the Possibility of a Just World Order: An Essay on Hegel's Universalism.* A volume in **Universal Justice**.

79. E.F. Kaelin, *Texts on Texts and Textuality: A Phenomenology of Literary Art*, edited by Ellen J. Burns.

80. Amihud Gilead, *Saving Possibilities: A Study in Philosophical Psychology*, A volume in **Philosophy and Psychology**.

81. André Mineau, *The Making of the Holocaust: Ideology and Ethics in the Systems Perspective.* A volume in **Holocaust and Genocide Studies**.

82. Howard P. Kainz, *Politically Incorrect Dialogues: Topics Not Discussed in Polite Circles.*

83. Veikko Launis, Juhani Pietarinen, and Juha Räikkä, Editors, *Genes and Morality: New Essays.* A volume in **Nordic Value Studies**.

84. Steven Schroeder, *The Metaphysics of Cooperation: A Study of F.D. Maurice.*

This book takes up the philosophical task described by Samuel Taylor Coleridge and F. D. Maurice as digging toward the common humanity that is the ground of value. As an essay in philosophy, this work is defined by time (its focal point is the nineteenth century), space (Britain), and persons (especially Maurice as contributor to social theory).

Steven Schroeder
(*photo by Herbert Schroeder*)

The VALUE INQUIRY BOOK SERIES (VIBS) is an international scholarly program that publishes philosophical books in all areas of value inquiry, including social and political thought, ethics, applied philosophy, feminism, personalism, religious values, values in education, medical and health values, values in science and technology, humanistic psychology, formal axiology, history of philosophy, post-communist thought, peace theory, law andsociety, and theory of culture.

ISBN 90-420-0776-1